From Freedom to Freedom

From Freedom to Freedom
African Roots in American Soil

A STUDENT'S GUIDE

Morris Johnson, William Primus, Sharon Thomas
MIAMI-DADE COMMUNITY COLLEGE

RANDOM HOUSE, NEW YORK

First Edition

9876543

Copyright © 1977 by Random House, Inc.

All rights reserved under International and Pan-American Copyright Conventions. No part of this book may be reproduced in any form or by any means, electronic or mechanical, including photocopying, without permission in writing from the publisher. All inquiries should be addressed to Random House, Inc., 201 East 50th Street, New York, N.Y. 10022. Published in the United States by Random House, Inc., and simultaneously in Canada by Random House of Canada Limited, Toronto.

ISBN 0-394-32078-6

Designed by J. M. Wall

Manufactured in the United States of America

INTRODUCTION

This course owes its existence to the book *Roots: The Saga of an American Family,* written by Alex Haley. Over a period of twelve years and a half-million miles of travel across three continents, Haley searched for documentation of his ancestral roots. In an astonishing feat of genealogical detective work, he found the name of his African ancestor—Kunta Kinte—and the exact location of Juffure, the village in The Gambia, West Africa, from which Kunta Kinte was abducted and brought to Maryland and sold to a Virginia planter.

As Haley undertook this genealogical dig to find his origins, he also unearthed a rich cultural heritage. His search and his findings are both reconstructed in *Roots.* Along with relating the story of his ancestors coming to this country, he also shares the history that was being made and the cultures that were being developed. He speaks not just to blacks, or to whites, but to all people of all races. The history and culture that Haley alludes to is the basis of the course.

This course may be structured somewhat differently from other courses you have taken. As you scan the course content you may initially feel that it is a history course. As you proceed through the course, however, you will find that its scope and depth cross many disciplines.

The course consists of several components and instructional materials. You may be exposed to all or to some of them. The instructional materials include (1) the book *Roots,* by Alex Haley, (2) the film series *Roots,* by Wolper Productions, (3) the selected readings, *From Freedom to Freedom,* and (4) the student guide, *From Freedom to Freedom.*

The purpose of the student guide is to lead you through the course. It contains ideas you will need to think about, but it will not by itself teach you all you need to know. The guide is divided into fifteen chapters, with subsections within each chapter. Each contains an *Overview* designed to give you an idea of what focus or subject matter is presented in that chapter. Next you will find a list of *Objectives* designed to let you know what you should be able to do as a result of studying that chapter. Then you will encounter *Major Themes,* which present the main ideas under investigation in the chapter. Next are the *Learning Activities* which guide your actions step by step to ensure that you will be able to accomplish the objectives. Then comes *Postevaluation,* a short, self-administered multiple-choice test that will help you evaluate your grasp of the major themes. The *Annotated Bibliography* will lead you to further exploration of any of the major themes. As you proceed through each section you will see maps and boxed information to give you additional insight into the major themes.

A special feature of the student guide is the *Continuity Table* at the beginning of the book. It is intended to provide a matrix of cross references between the student guide, selected readings, Haley's family tree, and the *Roots* story. The

Learning Activities section of each chapter refers you to the appropriate segment of the Continuity Table.

You will find that the *Roots* story not only provides sufficient information for the subject matter in the course, but also provides the basis for emotional stimulation and involvement in the course. The selected readings and the student guide serve as the academic complement to the book and the film production.

ACKNOWLEDGMENTS

Several people joined in the effort to develop this student guide. We are indebted to Alex Haley, whose book *Roots: The Saga of an American Family,* provided the basis for the project. Gratitude is expressed to the many others who assisted in the development of these materials: Ervin Lewis supervised editorial efforts; Susan Perrotti supervised the typing of the manuscript; John Lakey provided the cover art and illustrations; Usman Jobe, a student from The Gambia, provided invaluable cultural information on Africa. Finally, special gratitude is expressed to the faculty team, including Morris Johnson, Dr. William Primus, and Sharon Thomas, who were responsible for the instructional units in the guide, and to Wolper Productions, Inc.

Morris Johnson
Social Sciences and Director of Black Studies
CHAPTERS 2, 5, 6, 10, 12, and 13

William Primus
Political Science
CHAPTERS 2, 3, 7, 8, 9, and 14

Sharon Thomas
Education and Psychology
CHAPTERS 1, 2, 3, 4, 11, 15, and
Continuity Table

CONTENTS

The Continuity

The Continuity Table correlates the *Roots* story with the major themes presented in the student guide and the selected readings. As you encounter the *Roots* story either through reading the book or watching the film presentation, focus and reflect

Section	Student Guide/Selected Readings	The Family Tree
I	*Chapter One* Africa: Land of Diversity Land People	Omoro Kinte = Binta Kunta Kinte — — ⟶
II	*Chapter Two* Africa: Land of a Glorious Past Beginnings of man in Africa Ghana Mali Songhay	
III	*Chapter Three* Africa: A Rich Cultural Heritage I Social institutions Family Clan Tribe Political institutions Economic institutions	

Table

upon the items under the column entitled "The Roots Story." Then refer to the appropriate student guide chapters and selected readings for corresponding historical or cultural information.

Time Line	The Roots Story (Based on the book *Roots* and the film presentation)
1750: Kunta born in Juffure, The Gambia	A. The description of Juffure and the surrounding areas (the geographical location, the vegetation, etc.) B. The change in seasons from wet to dry and the ensuing changes in the lives of the people C. The physical features of Omoro, Binta, Kunta and others in the Mandinka tribe D. The allusions and references to people and tribes other than the Mandinka
	A. The role of the griot in the village of Juffure B. The story of Kunta's family history told to him by his grandmother, tracing his heritage to old Mali
	A. The family units within the Mandinka tribe living in Juffure B. The relationship between family members (siblings, children and parents) C. The universal paternal/maternal concern for children's welfare (shown by Omoro and Binta for Kunta's health upon learning of his fight with the lion) D. The makeup of the Kinte family compound E. The importance of Kunta's Kafo F. The formal way in which children were socialized in Mandinka society G. The role of manhood training and the lessons taught therein H. The distribution of labor among men, women, and children in Juffure I. The role of slaves in Mandinka society

Section	Student Guide/Selected Readings	The Family Tree
IV	*Chapter Four* Africa: A Rich Cultural Heritage II African languages African art African religion	
V	*Chapter Five* Africa to America: The Beginnings of Slavery Pre-Columbian presence Slavery Comparative approach	Kunta Kinte ⟶

Time Line	The Roots Story (Based on the book *Roots* and the film presentation)
	J. The judicial role held by the Council of Elders in Juffure
	K. The importance of the seating arrangements at the Council of Elders
	A. The influence of Islam on the lives of the Mandinka and particularly on Kunta
	B. The rituals performed at births, deaths, weddings, harvest times, etc.
	C. The importance of the circumcision ritual
	D. The new roles Kunta was expected to assume after manhood training
	E. The variety of instruments and the unique function of the drums
	F. The multiple functions of art in the daily lives of the Mandinka
	G. The ritual performed for those Mandinka captured by the white man
	H. The different languages spoken both by the Mandinka and other tribes
1767: Kunta captured into slavery	A. The warnings given to Kunta and his brothers about the Toubob (white man)
	B. Omoro's explanation of black African participation in procuring slaves for whites
	C. Kunta's capture by slave procurers
	D. The tools of slavery presented on the Lord Ligoner—neckrings, chains, shackles and thumbscrews, manacles
	E. The anguish of Kunta's family upon realizing he had been captured
	F. The conduct of the slave ship crew in preparation for a cargo of slaves
	G. The way in which slave cargo is regarded in the same light as nonhuman cargo
	H. The Christian justification for slavery offered by the slave ship's captain

Section	Student Guide/Selected Readings	The Family Tree
VI	*Chapter Six* Slavery: The Birth of the Industrial Revolution Industrial order African contributions to the industrial order Triangular trade Africa and the Industrial Revolution	

Time Line	The Roots Story (Based on the book *Roots* and the film presentation)
	I. Kunta's reaction to being branded
	J. Kunta's attempt to hold on to the memory of Juffure as his ship leaves for the New World
	K. The atrocities of the middle passage—fixed melancholy
	L. Slave ship captain's attempt to conduct a Christian ship and his subsequent defeat
	M. The coping mechanisms developed by the enslaved in an attempt to maintain sanity and survive the middle passage
	N. The abuse of the slave women by the ship's crew
	O. The daily record kept of cargo losses (slave deaths)
	P. The village which the slaves form in the hold of the ship
	Q. The communication code established between men and women on the ship
	R. The completion of the business transaction as slave cargo is delivered in Annapolis
	S. The slave seasoning process
	T. Kunta's reaction to the slave auction
	U. Kunta's reaction to alien white culture
	V. Kunta's reaction to New World blacks who acquiesce to their masters
	W. The dehumanization of the auctioning process
	X. The regard for the natural order of things by the whites (the auction, chains, etc.)
	Y. Kunta's response to his new slave name, "Toby"
	A. The upkeep of the ship after slaves had been unloaded in preparation for new cargo (tobacco) to go to England
	B. The predictions made that cotton would eventually amass unforetold profits
	C. Master's rationale for reluctance to change crops from tobacco to cotton
	D. The number of African blacks in the New World (representing economic loss to Africa)
	E. Celebrations surrounding a good harvest which indicate more trade and greater profit and increased need for slaves

Section	Student Guide/Selected Readings	The Family Tree
VII	*Chapter Seven* Slavery: Its Development in Colonial America The political rights of white indentured servants The indentured status of blacks in Virginia and Maryland The trends that led to de jure slavery	
VIII	*Chapter Eight* Slavery: As Practiced in the Thirteen Colonies Slavery in colonial America Impact of Quakers on slavery Slave revolts in early America	
IX	*Chapter Nine* Revolutionary Philosophy: Its Impact on Slavery The roots of the American Revolution The impact of the writings of John Locke Jefferson's attack on slavery Black contributions during the Revolutionary era Black literary figures during the Revolutionary era	

Time Line	The Roots Story (Based on the book *Roots* and the film presentation)
	A. Kunta's perceptions and comparisons of New World blacks and the dehumanization they underwent as slavery developed in colonial America
	B. Kunta's perception of how blacks lost their sense of identity
	C. The rationale offered for not allowing slaves to beat drums
	D. Kunta's defeat as he succumbs to the masters as other blacks had done
	E. Kunta's attempt to deal with the inconsistency of befriending Fiddler
	F. The descriptions of poor whites and their relationship to blacks
1770: Boston Massacre, death of Crispus Attucks	G. Kunta's reaction to seeing whites subjected to slave treatment
	H. The description of white indentureds
	I. The comparison of the fate of white indentureds to the fate of black slaves
	A. Fiddler's description of the colonial composition of this country to Kunta
	B. The slaves' methods of finding out and relaying news about slavery developments in other colonies
1775: Battle of Bunker Hill, in which Peter Salem and Salem Poor excelled	A. Kunta's reaction to whites' crying "Give me liberty, or give me death"
	B. Reactions on slave row to the news of Bunker Hill
	C. Slaves' methods of gathering and sharing news about the Revolution
1776: Declaration of Independence	D. Slave descriptions of George Washington, Quakers, The Anti–Slavery Society, Lord Dunmore
	E. Slaves' reaction to Lord Dunmore's decree
1783: Official end of Revolutionary War	F. Slaves' reaction to learning of the July 4, 1776 Declaration of Independence
	G. Bell's delivery speech that the Revolution was over

Section	Student Guide/Selected Readings	The Family Tree
X	*Chapter Ten* Plantation Life: Emergence of a Culture 　　Daily life 　　Slave speech 　　Music, dance, stories 　　Religion	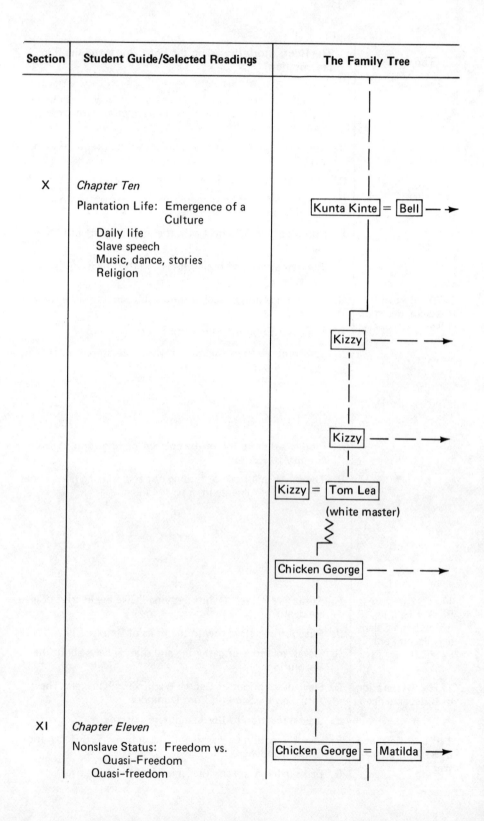
XI	*Chapter Eleven* Nonslave Status: Freedom vs. Quasi-Freedom 　　Quasi-freedom	

The Family Tree:

Kunta Kinte = Bell →

Kizzy → → →

Kizzy → → →

Kizzy = Tom Lea
(white master)

Chicken George → → →

Chicken George = Matilda →

Time Line	The Roots Story (Based on the book *Roots* and the film presentation)
1787: Slavery legitimatized by the Constitution	
1789: Kunta married Bell in Spotsylvania County, Virginia	A. The differences between the privileges granted to house slaves and field slaves
	B. Kunta's reaction to the intimate friendships between black and white children
	C. Fiddler's explanation of how and why young children learned to play instruments
	D. The description of slave row
	E. The comparison of Bell's cabin to the others
1790: Born	F. The importance of traveling passes and other restrictions—black codes
1791: Haitian Revolution	G. Slave speech and rhetoric
1800: Gabriel Prosser uprising	H. Kunta's initial reaction and reluctance to learn English
	I. The slaves' communication system among plantations
	J. Kunta's reaction to the slave diet—particularly pork
1805: Kizzy sold to Tom Lea in Caswell County, North Carolina	K. Slave means of relaxation
	L. Intimate communities that formed on the various slave rows
	M. Slave marriage rituals
	N. The function of religion on slave row
	O. Kunta's reaction to the "O Lawd" religion of the slaves
	P. Kunta's desperate attempts to hold on to Africanisms and pass them to his child
1806: Born in Caswell, County, North Carolina	Q. Bell's reaction to Africanisms
	R. Perpetuation of the oral tradition through storytelling
	S. Slaves kept in line by the overseers' whips
	T. Descriptions of slaves' clothing, diet, recreation, etc.
	U. The breakup of slave families—Kizzy sold away from Kunta and Bell
	A. The tragedy of Fiddler's attempt to buy his freedom
1827: Married in Caswell County, North Carolina	B. The slave accounts told of slaves who fled northward to freedom

Section	Student Guide/Selected Readings	The Family Tree
	Economic life among free blacks Family life among free blacks Education for free blacks Free blacks and Western expansion Free blacks and American wars	
XII	*Chapter Twelve* Abolition: The Antislavery Crusade Gradualism and colonization Militant abolitionism Black abolitionists Slavery debates	Tom Murray Tom Murray = Irene ⟶ (Half Cherokee)
XIII	*Chapter Thirteen* Civil War: The Beginning of a New Era Lincoln as emancipator The Blue, the Gray, the black The slave as freedman	Cynthia ⟶

Time Line	The Roots Story (Based on the book *Roots* and the film presentation)
	C. Chicken George's contact with free blacks and their impact upon him
	D. Chicken George's plan to buy his family's freedom
	E. Accounts of free blacks in the North fighting against slavery
	F. Accounts of free blacks who traveled, lecturing and recounting how they became free
	G. The slave apprenticeships that prepared them for work as free blacks
	H. The relationship between slave and free blacks
1833: Born in Caswell County, North Carolina	A. The accounts and reports of slaves revolting against masters
	B. Tom Lea's violent reaction to news of slave revolts
	C. Role of the Quakers and the Anti–Slavery Society
1855: Chicken George sent to England to train fighting cocks	D. Tom's accounts and descriptions to his family about Sojourner Truth, Harriet Tubman, and other leaders
	E. Tom's account of the bitterness whites felt toward northern abolitionists
1859: Married in Alamance County, North Carolina	F. The description of "typical" white abolitionists
1861: Civil War begins	A. The news that comes to Tom's shop about the upcoming war
1863: Emancipation Proclamation	B. Incident which forces Tom to work for Confederate Army
	C. Tom's accounts to his family of specific battles, incidents and ultimate surrender
	D. The gathering master calls to inform them of their freedom
1865: War ends	E. Slaves' responses and reactions to freedom
1871: Born in Alamance County, North Carolina	

Section	Student Guide/Selected Readings	The Family Tree
XIV	*Chapter Fourteen* Political Compromise: The Nadir of Black Americans Black political gains during Reconstruction The Compromise of 1877 Extralegal and illegal methods of intimidation The educational philosophy of Booker T. Washington The alternative educational philosophy of W. E. B. Du Bois	Cynthia = Will Palmer ––→ Bertha – – – – →
XV	*Chapter Fifteen* America: A Cultural Exchange African retentions in language and folklore African retentions in art African retentions in music Black American contributions to the development of America Exploration Economy Inventions and Discoveries Democracy Contributions to the Arts	Bertha = Simon Haley – –→ Alex – – – →

Time Line	The Roots Story (Based on the book *Roots* and the film presentation)
1873: Murray's family moves to Henning, Tennessee	A. The attacks of the night riders on Tom and his family B. The response of the law to the night riders' attacks C. The response of the federal troops to the night riders' attacks
1893: Married in Henning, Tennessee	D. The ultimate response of the Murray family to the attack of the night riders E. The desire of the family to make its own way
1894: Will Palmer opened Tennessee's first black owned lumber company	F. The voyage and feelings expressed as the family treks to Tennessee
1895: Born in Henning, Tennessee	
1920: Married	A. The entire Roots Story—especially the following: B. Kunta's reactions and thoughts about assimilated blacks he found in the New World C. The various jobs of the slaves and the devices they created to make their lives and work easier
1921: Born in Ithaca, New York	D. The way slaves spent their free time E. Specific incidents or people that made Kunta recall life in Juffure F. The mortar and pestle Kunta carried for Bell G. The drummer and his interaction with Kunta H. The work of the slave family and how they provided for the development of a southern leisure class I. Black participation in the Revolutionary and Civil wars J. The response of the whites to the blacks who participated

From Freedom to Freedom

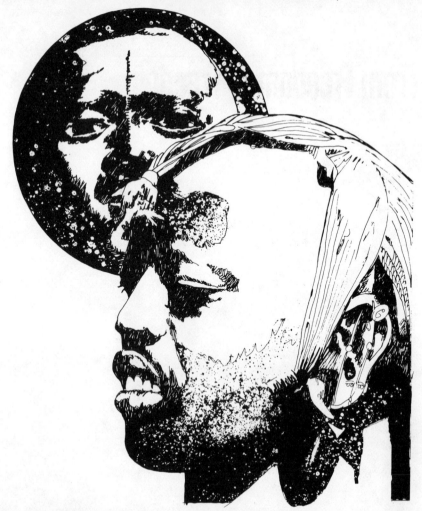

CHAPTER ONE

AFRICA:
Land of Diversity

Knowledge is like a garden; if it is not cultivated, it cannot
be harvested. (AFRICAN PROVERB)

OVERVIEW

"Diverse" is probably as appropriate a word as one could use to describe the continent of Africa. This is true of its people and of its geography.

The continent rises out of the waters of the Atlantic Ocean, the Indian Ocean, the Mediterranean Sea, and the Red Sea. Its vast land mass spans 5,000 miles, from its northernmost points on the Mediterranean to its southern extremities near the Cape of Good Hope.

Africa is shaped somewhat like a question mark. This is indeed fitting, not only because the future is unknowable but because much of Africa's past, including civilizations that may have surpassed those of any other continent in their time, is yet to be told.

This chapter—and entire course—seeks to trace and identify Africa's remarkable diversity: its beauty, its natural resources, its geographic history, its many and different peoples.

It is essential to begin with the continent's physiography, for herein lies the roots of African history and culture. Its topography ranges from deserts to dense forests and snow-capped mountains. It is marked with rivers, waterfalls, and immense lakes. Its vegetation, as might be expected, is as varied as its climate. Yet all these extremes are exceeded, perhaps, by the astounding variety of its human population.

Approximately 374 million persons live in Africa. There are many colors and races, representing several cultures, many languages, and a rich tapestry of beliefs and styles of life. These differences contribute to energy and progress and occasionally to misunderstanding and lack of cooperation.

OBJECTIVES

As a result of studying this chapter, you should be able to:
1. Identify the major geographical regions of Africa by locating and labeling them on an outline map.
2. Identify the vegetational zones of Africa by locating and labeling them on an outline map.
3. Identify the climatic zones of Africa by locating and labeling them on an outline map.
4. Differentiate between savanna, rain forests, and desert by describing the characteristic appearance of each one.
5. Identify the five major rivers in Africa by locating them on a map.
6. Distinguish between Africa's diverse populations by describing the characteristics of each of the six classifications of people.
7. Illustrate the relationship between Africa's people and land by describing how the land (climate and vegetation) affects the lives of the people.

MAJOR THEMES

LAND

Africa is the second largest continent. With a land area of 11.7 million square miles, it is more than three times the size of the continental United States. Africa lies squarely across the equator, with its northern and southern extremes almost equidistant from the equator. With 9 million square miles in the tropical zone, it is the most tropical of the continents.

Twenty percent of the African continent consists of rain forests. These humid, forested lands straddle the equator and appear also in the coastal areas of western Africa. As the name indicates, these areas have the heaviest rainfall. The forests vary from an extreme of heavy foliage to wooded areas that are almost open enough to be called savanna. Between these two extremes are many types of woodland.

More than 40 percent of Africa consists of savannas or grasslands. The grasslands vary in density from scattered trees, bushes, and short grass in dry regions to grass that grows 6 to 8 feet high in the wetter areas. Africa's wild game and pastoral societies are found in the grasslands.

Farther from the equator on both sides are the dry lands of Africa. Forty percent of the continent is covered by deserts. There are three main desert areas: in the south is the Kalahari Desert, and in the north, the Sahara; there are also deserts along the coast of the Red Sea and Somalia. Most of the desert area is barren and desolate, but some areas are covered with shrubs and enough grass to make them suitable for limited grazing.

With some exceptions, the climate on both sides of the equator in Africa is parallel from east to west. This mirror image is upset in the eastern part of the continent by highland areas. Some of the highlands are steep and mountainous; others are high, rolling plateaus. In these highlands, the climate may be quite cool and temperate. The vegetation will vary from humid forest or savanna at the foothills to large mountain ranges.

The climate in Africa depends primarily on the winds, the position of the sun, and the altitude. Most of Africa has two seasons, alternating between a long dry period and a shorter wet, or rainy, period. There is a stretch of land along the equator that has two wet seasons and two dry seasons during the year. The desert areas receive less than 5 inches of rain per year; some areas may receive no rain for several years.

Africa's highlands and lowlands spawned a historically important topographical feature: a series of rivers that develop into waterfalls before spilling into the sea. Five major rivers are usually identified. The longest of Africa's rivers is the Nile, which is about 4,100 miles long. Africa's second longest river is the Congo. It runs for 2,718 miles. The Niger River is 2,600 miles long and is the third longest river in Africa. At 1,600 miles, the Zambezi River is the fourth longest. Fifth in length, 1,300 miles, is the Orange River. These rivers are navigable for long

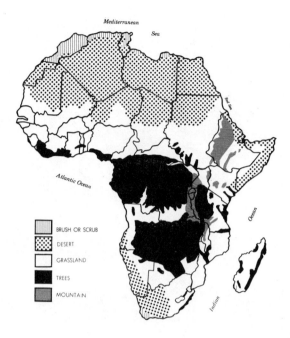

stretches in the interior of the continent, but waterfalls usually impede penetration of the continent from the outside.

As a result, Africa is a continent with ample means for transport and communication via the great river systems and across the large plains. The desert areas have always been difficult to cross, presumably, but with greater rainfall in the past, they once supported many more people than they presently do. The rain forest has almost always sustained large concentrations of population. Africa's weather fosters a pastoral more than an agricultural economy. Africa's shifting cultivation and erratic harvests have restricted its populations, as well as encouraged political decentralization.

PEOPLE

The task of classifying Africa's people is made difficult by insufficient data; confusion among racial, linguistic, and cultural terminology; intermarriages, migrations, and conquests with the resulting mixing of peoples.

Ethnic classifications of African peoples have been based on physical characteristics as well as languages. More recently, data concerning blood groups are being used to clarify Africa's ethnic complexity. As new data become available, traditional concepts of racial development may well change. Six classifications are generally used to describe Africa's principal population segments. They are:

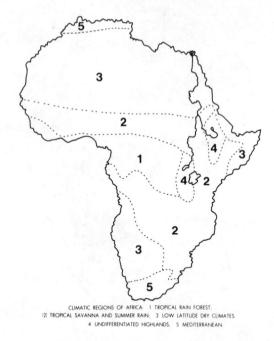

CLIMATIC REGIONS OF AFRICA: 1 TROPICAL RAIN FOREST;
(2) TROPICAL SAVANNA AND SUMMER RAIN; 3 LOW LATITUDE DRY CLIMATES;
4 UNDIFFERENTIATED HIGHLANDS; 5 MEDITERRANEAN.

1. *Negrillos,* also called Pygmies, who live in the equatorial rain forest areas;
2. *Bushmen and Hottentots;* the Bushmen live in the Kalahari Desert, the Hottentots live in southwestern Africa;
3. *Hamites,* who are white people occupying Ethiopia and much of the Sahara;
4. *"True" Negroes,* who live in western Africa and the Sudan;
5. *Hamiticized Negroes,* who are the several groups of people (Nilotes, Nilo Hamites, and Bantu) produced from the mixing of Negro and Hamitic ancestry;
6. *Semites,* who are the Arabs, living mostly in Egypt and northern Africa.

   In addition, many persons of European and Asian descent live in Africa, most of them along the northern coast or in the south. Over prolonged periods of time, many people of these backgrounds have intermarried, creating even further mixtures.

LEARNING ACTIVITIES

To accomplish the objectives of this chapter, you should do the following:
A. Study the chapter Overview.
B. Read the Major Themes.
C. Read Chapter One in the anthology.
D. Examine carefully Section I of the Continuity Table.

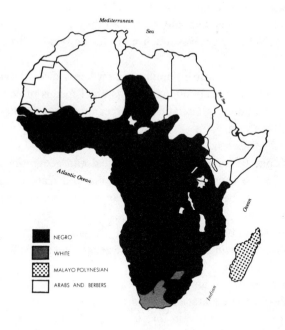

E. Answer these questions.
   1. What impact did geography and climatic zones have on the development of African culture?
   2. What accounts for such wide diversity among African peoples?

POSTEVALUATION

To check your learning, select the most appropriate answer to each of the following questions:
1. Vegetation in Africa is dense. The nature of the undergrowth varies depending directly on
   a. the number of animals that thrive there.
   b. the different minerals found in the soil.
   c. the amount of rainfall.
   d. the number of irrigation rivers.
2. One could infer that the reason why the earliest African history of which we are aware is found in the Sahara Desert is because
   a. years ago the coasts and the southern parts of Africa were heavily populated.
   b. in ancient times the southern and central Sahara were probably the most heavily populated.

   c. the Sahara and Kalahari were sparsely populated.
   d. the area once was lush and supported an industrious population.
3. Since the Sahara Desert was much more fertile two or three thousand years ago, it
   a. could support extensive populations on herds of cattle grazing there.
   b. is quite likely that commerce was its chief means of economy.
   c. forced its human inhabitants to retreat into the savanna.
   d. all of the above.
4. Classifying Africa's population is
   a. easily done because of clear-cut political and geographical boundaries.
   b. easily done because of obvious skin color and feature distinctions.
   c. difficult to do because of confusion among racial, linguistic, and cultural terminology.
   d. difficult to do because of tribalism.
5. Which of the following is incorrect? The geographical distribution of Africa's people is as follows:
   a. Bushmen in South and East Africa.
   b. Pygmies in the equatorial rain forest areas.
   c. whites in the interior rain forests.
   d. Negroes in the Sahara and the savanna north of the rain forest.
(For correct answers, see ANSWER KEY.)

ANNOTATED BIBLIOGRAPHY

Bohannon, Paul. *Africa and Africans.* New York: The Natural History Press, 1964. An easily read book that attempts to put African culture in modern perspective for Western readers by examining African facts and the Western myths that have obscured them. Chapter 3 considers the size, shape, and geological composition of the African continent.
Church, R. J. H. *Africa and the Islands.* New York: Wiley, 1971. A scholarly account of African history and the history of the surrounding islands; treats history region by region; has an excellent selection of maps and graphs.
Traditional Africa in a Modern World. Field Enterprises Educational Corporation, 1973. A pamphlet that summarizes African history. The articles within it are easily read and very well illustrated.

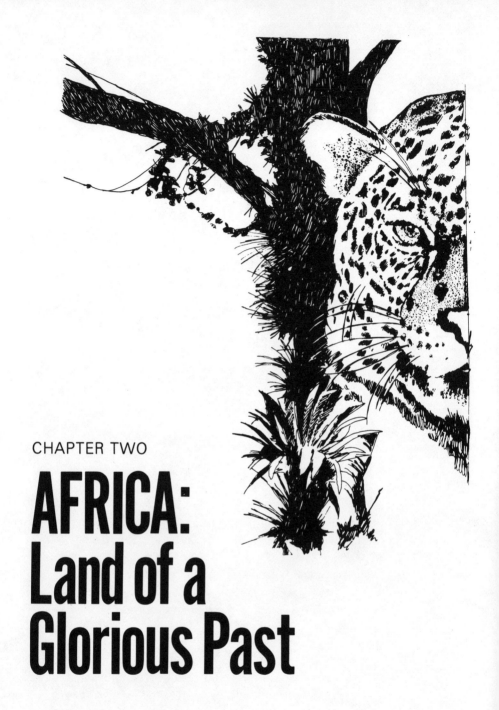

CHAPTER TWO

AFRICA: Land of a Glorious Past

If you know the beginning well, the end will not trouble you. (AFRICAN PROVERB)

OVERVIEW

Africa was probably the birthplace of all mankind. To have an accurate picture and a true understanding of the human story, one must begin with the history of Africa.

The study of African history is not new. Until recently, however, African history was presented in a distorted fashion. The American version relegated it to minor importance. The European version tended to be a colonial history that focused on the Europeans in Africa rather than on Africans.

The result of African history's being recorded from non-African perspectives was a negative, heavily stereotyped view of Africa. The images most people had were those of Tarzan, fierce natives, lions, great green greasy rivers, savages, and so forth. Or perhaps the images were very romantic but equally unrealistic, portraying exciting safaris, treks through dense jungles, silvery velds, undulating savannas, and parched deserts. As Africa moves into the foreground, there is a wider awareness that it was never a changeless, barbaric continent, but one with a glorious past that has undergone changes similar to the changes in human events as a whole.

This chapter attempts to illuminate that glorious past. The emphasis is on what has often and erroneously been called darkest Africa, because actually it is a continent where civilizations rose and fell, leaving valuable contributions to the rest of the world. In this Africa, Islam and Christianity fought other religious beliefs and oftentimes each other. To this Africa came people from the rest of the world—traders, followed by explorers and invaders, most of whom were in search of Africa's jewels, gold, ivory, diamonds, and the "black gold" of slavery.

Historians now recognize this past as valid and indispensable to the overall history of man. They are tossing away the old maps of Africa and the old colonial history and are recognizing that African history is experiencing a rebirth. Previously, it was believed that one could not study precolonial Africa because nothing had happened or been recorded before the colonial period. This was a mistaken view, because societies that were nonliterate usually had institutions for preserving and transmitting traditions orally.

An integral part of this rebirth in African history is the broadening of the field of historiography to include archeology. With the new dating techniques—radiocarbon dating and insights into stratification—archeologists can validate much of African history. Through the study of languages (including the oral tradition and reading old documents), linguists can shed new light on African history.

This new approach to the past is not just the uncovering of new data about Africa. It involves raising new questions and adopting new attitudes. It is an attempt to reduce or eliminate ethnocentric bias by asking new questions about the dynamics of African societies. Such questions concern the recurrent patterns of change that may have been different from those of the West. They concern how and why various African societies reacted differently to the Western challenge.

Much work remains to be done to recover all of African history. But with each new fact reconstructed, there develops a more complete history of all mankind.

OBJECTIVES

As a result of studying this chapter, you should be able to:
1. Describe man's beginnings in Africa by listing the major evolutionary developments as recorded by anthropologists.
2. Relate the significance of trade to Ghana's economic prosperity by identifying trade goods and trade routes.
3. Discuss Ghana's judicial system by describing the king's role as administrator of justice.
4. Illustrate the leadership skills of early African emperors by summarizing the contributions of Sundiator and those of Askia Mohammed.
5. Analyze the impact of Islam upon the ruling kingdom of Mali by stating its effect upon the kings and upon the people.
6. Analyze the significance of historic pilgrimages to Mecca by contrasting the motives of Mansa Musa's pilgrimage in 1324 with those of Askia Mohammed in 1497.
7. Assess the impact that modern traders had upon the development of ancient kingdoms by describing specific changes that took place.
8. Describe the development of the judicial systems in the ancient kingdoms by identifying Islamic legal contributions.

MAJOR THEMES
THE BEGINNINGS OF MAN IN AFRICA

Most archeologists now believe that the birthplace of man was somewhere on the African continent, probably south of the Sahara Desert. Raymond Dart made the first discovery of fossil primate remains in southern Africa in 1924. He uncovered the greater part of a juvenile skull. It showed characteristics that, in Dart's opinion, placed it midway between the apes and the oldest definitely identifiable human fossils. He called it "Australopithecus africanus" (South African Ape). Many rejected Dart's implications and theories of Africa's being man's birthplace. The Dart findings were supported when zoologist Robert Bloom unearthed an adult ape-man in a cave near Johannesburg, South Africa. Digs that have been underway in eastern Africa since 1959 have further confirmed Dart's theories and increased our knowledge of early man. Louis and Mary Leakey and their son, Richard, working at Olduvai Gorge in Tanzania, unearthed several finds. From these fossils of manlike creatures and their stone tools and artifacts, scientists have concluded that the ancestor of both man and ape came into being in Africa about 20 million years ago.

About 35,000 years ago, man as we know him, Homo sapiens, appeared. Many bits and pieces in the puzzle are still missing, so the story is incomplete. Yet scientists feel relatively sure that, by about 14,000 B.C., man was well entrenched in Africa; and the man-apes had become extinct. Man had already developed family and community life. He used relatively sophisticated tools and weapons, he knew how to gather and use plants for food, and he knew how to make and use fire.

As the years passed, important changes took place in Africa's climate and vegetation that affected man's development. The Sahara Desert, for example, once lush and green, became very dry and brought profound changes in the lives of the people in the area. When the Sahara was verdant, the inhabitants were fisherfolk and cattlemen. But as the land grew arid, lifestyles were altered to meet the new conditions. Most of the population migrated in pursuit of a water supply and became farmers and herders. Everyone did not migrate; some stayed behind, adapting to the rigors of the desert, and became nomads.

Those who migrated south of the Sahara found savannas where farming was possible, and the economy became agricultural. Some had a knowledge of iron-working, but there was a shortage of salt. So trade in salt and gold was established between desert area and savanna.

Living in the savanna century after century, the inhabitants had developed governments, customs, and laws. The majority of the population was the product of racial intermixture—yet the different tribal and cultural entities coexisted peaceably. During this time large, regal, and powerful kingdoms emerged under African kings.

GHANA

Ghana was prosperous. Three major facts can account for this. First was the geographic location. Ghana served as a relay point for trade between western and northern Africa. The northern African demand for gold and the western African demand for salt were the primary reasons why the city of Kunbi-Kunbi became Ghana's important commercial center during the eleventh century. The second major fact was Ghana's extensive agricultural pursuits. The third was Ghana's conversion to Islam. By the eleventh century, the leaders of Ghana embraced the Islamic faith in order to increase their political and socioeconomic powers.

Under the Sisse dynasty, early in the eleventh century, Ghana reached the height of its power. In 1062, Emperor Tenkamein collected taxes and tributes from provincial traders; held court in a fortified castle which was beautified by royal artists; and personally administered justice, bestowed honors on worthy subjects, and punished those who incurred his disfavor.

The decline of the Ghanaian Empire began in 1076 after an invasion by Muslim fanatics called the Almoravids. The Almoravids caused religious strife which

1. *Raymond Dart*, as mentioned in key concepts, found and named the Taung child *Australopithecus africanus* (Southern Ape) in 1924. Today some anthropologists use the name *Homo africanus*.
2. *Mary Leakey*, who found the first skull of *Australopithecus boisei* (at first named *Zinjanthropus*) and also the first complete skull of Proconsul, is an authority on the stone tools of ancient man.
3. *Louis Leakey* described the Olduvan Pebble culture in 1931, named and described *Zinjanthropus* in 1959, *Homo habilis* in 1960, together with early Acheulian stone tools, and found the earliest known fossils of *Homo erectus* at Olduvai.
4. *Richard Leakey*, son of the late Louis and Mary Leakey, traces early man and stone tools back 2,500,000 years in the Lake Rudolph region. His discovery of a skull known by its collection number "ER 1470" indicates a large-brained man which preceded *Australopithecus*.

ultimately undermined the kingdom. Ghana's decline was also hastened by a series of droughts. Weakened by these destructive circumstances, Ghana was conquered and destroyed by the end of the twelfth century.

MALI

Mali, under the leadership of Sundiata Keitagan from 1230 to 1255, and Mansa Uli, Sundiata's successor, emerged as the imperial successor to Ghana. A later successor, Emperor Mansa Musa, was the most prominent Malian emperor. He continued the geographic consolidation of Mali by incorporating a large part of the central and western regions of the western Sudan into a single system of law and order. Under Mansa, Mali attained the highest level of its political and socioeconomic development.

Mansa Musa used his Islamic pilgrimage to Mecca in 1324 to display the tremendous wealth of Mali to the rest of the Islamic world and to attract new trade. This historic pilgrimage had an entourage of thousands, plus 80 camels bearing 24,000 pounds of gold. Mansa Musa brought Abu Ishak, a distinguished Arabian poet and architect, back with him to Mali. Abu Ishak later supervised the building of mosques in Timbuktu, Jenne, and Gao, the intellectual centers of Mali.

Mansa Musa died in 1332, and was succeeded by Suleiman. Under the latter's rule, the economy continued to flourish; trade relations expanded, and there was political stability. However, early in the fourteenth century, Mali began to exhibit signs of decline and disintegration. Repeated attacks by the developing, powerful kingdoms of Songhay reduced Mali to a small subject state.

Eventually, the people of Songhay were able to defeat their oppressors. The first ruling dynasty of Songhay was that of the Sonnis. Seventeen kings reigned in this dynasty. The last was Sonni Ali, who raised Songhay to the position of the most

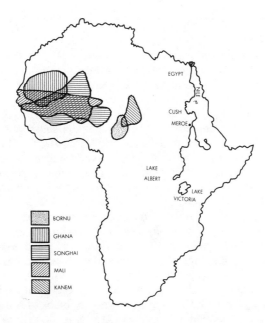

powerful and developed state in western Africa. The Sonnis dynasty was overthrown by Askia Mohammed, Songhay's greatest ruler. Askia's rule brought increased contact with the Arab world and the conquest of neighboring territories.

Timbuktu became a major city in the empire. A cultural center, the city was filled with scholars, musicians, judges, doctors, and clinics. The University of Sankore in Timbuktu offered courses in law, Islam, literature, natural sciences, and medicine. Students from all over Africa and the Arab world attended the university.

Askia continued to improve upon his empire by taking a pilgrimage to Mecca in 1497. Unlike the ostentatious display of wealth by Mansa Musa, Askia's pilgrimage promoted intellectual exchange among doctors and scholars in the Arab world. Askia was able to upgrade the administration of government, to revise the codified laws, and to raise education standards in his empire. Gao, Walata, and Jenne became major cities and intellectual centers like Timbuktu.

Askia was dethroned by his eldest son and eventual civil wars and unsuccessful military expeditions caused the empire to decline. Invasions by Moors and Moroccans brought about the total destruction of Songhay early in the sixteenth century.

ISLAM

Islam made its entrance into Egypt in A.D. 639. Within a century, through conversion and conquest, Islam had spread over all of northern Africa. The

Islam and Slavery

Slavery had existed in Africa for many centuries. With the coming of Islam to the Sudan, the slave trade to northern Africa increased; Islam sanctioned the enslaving of "infidels" and held that such servitude was just. Also, Islam rejected indigenous African religion as being godless and primitive. Black Africans who were "pagan" were viewed as fair game for bondage. Black slaves worked under deplorable conditions in the salt mines of the dreary village of Taghaza (the salt trade was controlled by Arabs). Thus, the Islamic world view divided mankind into two groups: Muslims and non-Muslims. However, this division did not save black Muslims from being sold into slavery. One Arabic scholar stated that a pagan's conversion to Islam did not automatically give him freedom.

Bilad al Sudan means "land of the blacks." Ancient Arabic literature is full of terms used to describe the varieties of skin colors. In many drawings of Islamic culture, black slaves are shown performing menial tasks. Arabs used names like Nuba, Beja, and Zanj to describe black peoples south of the Sahara. Extremely important was the negative connotation connected with the term Zanj, which was used only in reference to the Bantu-speaking black people of eastern Africa. (Since they were very black, the Arabs held that they were good for nothing but slavery.) It is interesting to note that Zanj was never used in reference to Sudan blacks or to Ethiopians. At the same time, black Africans were integrated into most aspects of Arab society.

intrusion of the Arabs into northern Africa set the stage for increased contacts between black Africa and the Islamic world. This contact between Arabs and Africans enhanced the quality of life for both groups.

Islam in its initial stages came to western Africa by means of trade. Muslim traders occupied a section of the chief city of Old Ghana. The king soon realized the importance of accommodating Arabs at his court. Many of them served as scribes or as ambassadors to distant Islamic countries. They collected information and, in general, improved the efficiency of business transactions of the royal house. At the same time, written Arabic was introduced, thereby aiding literacy and the beginnings of a recorded history. The building of mosques and the growth of new towns were all a part of the new wealth being forged in the black Sudan.

The impact of Islam did not destroy the traditional cultures of western Africa. In many instances the old and the new existed side by side. The people of western Africa remained rooted in traditional beliefs and customs; they merely grafted a thin layer of Islam over the existing religions. Islam was not always well received. Many rejected Islam and resisted it, thereby blocking its expansion into the interior of black Africa. Islam, nonetheless, left imprints upon the Sudan. The Muslims introduced a new moral code which forbade human sacrifice. Islamic legal codes emphasized that individuals should be trained as judges, thus usurping the authority of village elders who traditionally decided matters of justice and disputes. Increased trade with the Muslim world gave the people of the Sudan an international outlook. Lastly, Islam aided the growth of literacy, because those who considered themselves good Muslims felt duty-bound to be able to read the Koran.

LEARNING ACTIVITIES

To accomplish the objectives of this chapter, you should do the following:
A. Study the chapter Overview.
B. Read the Major Themes.
C. Read Chapter Two in the anthology.
D. Examine Section II of the Continuity Table.
E. Answer these questions.
   1. How does the evolutionary thesis of mankind's development reinforce or contradict your personal beliefs about man's origin?
   2. How have archeological finds contributed to our knowledge of early man?
   3. In what ways were the trade relations between the Arab world and Ghana profitable to both areas?
   4. What evidence suggests there was a sophisticated judicial system in early Ghana?
   5. What specific leadership skills were characteristic of the reigns?
   6. Why was the response of the people of Mali to Islam different from the response of the leadership?
   7. Why were these differences important?
F. (Optional) Answer these questions based on the *Roots* story.
   1. How was Kunta informed of his history and his ancestral past?
   2. How and by whom was the village of Juffure established?
   3. How did Islam directly affect Kunta's upbringing, thoughts, and actions?

POSTEVALUATION

To check your learning, select the most appropriate answer to each of the following questions:
1. At one time it was believed that Africa had no history of any significance. This perspective was based on
   a. a belief that history exists only when there are written records and archeological remains to document it.
   b. the belief that very little that happened in Africa was worth noting.
   c. the belief that the only history of Africa was that which the Mediterranean and European explorers and colonists had written.
   d. all of the above.
   e. only (a) and (c) are correct.
2. This perspective about African history has changed because
   a. documents and archeology are the best sources of historical knowledge.
   b. the oral tradition is recognized as accurate historical documentation.

      c. other disciplines have contributed to knowledge about Africa's past.

      d. all of the above.

      e. only (b) and (c) are correct.

3. At the present time, which of the following statements conclusively supports the theory that Africa was the birthplace of mankind?

      a. Archeological findings in Asia establish that man and other animals could not have existed there simultaneously.

      b. Archeological findings in Africa date further back than those found in Asia.

      c. the belief that Africa is the center-most continent and thus would have had the most conducive conditions for human life.

4. The Trans-Saharan trade was prosperous in the days of the ancient kingdoms because

      a. there were stable settlements to serve as marketplaces for the two valuable products—gold and salt.

      b. the people whose economy had been based on grazing were forced to adapt to trade in order to survive.

      c. horses and camels were readily available to transport gold and salt goods back and forth.

      d. life in the once-lush Sahara was so well organized that adaptation to commercial economy was easily accomplished.

      e. all of the above.

5. The once-great empire of Ghana gradually declined from its position of prominence. This decline was precipitated by

      a. a decrease in the availability of gold necessary for commerce.

      b. attacks by a band of people known as the Almoravids.

      c. discovery of gold deposits in areas of North Africa.

      d. all of the above.

(For correct answers, see ANSWER KEY.)

ANNOTATED BIBLIOGRAPHY

Bohannon, Paul. *Africa and Africans.* New York: The Natural History Press, 1964. An easily read book that presents African history from a modern perspective.

Davidson, Basil. *Africa in History.* New York: Macmillan, 1969. A scholarly presentation of Africa's evolutionary development from ancient civilization, conquest, colonial rule, and liberation.

Davidson, Basil. *The African Genius.* Boston: Little, Brown, 1969. An empirical introduction to the study of Africa's cultural and social history.

Franklin, John Hope. *From Slavery to Freedom.* New York: Knopf, 1974. A definitive study of the history of American blacks from ancient African beginnings to the present.

Joseph, Alvin Jr. (ed.). *The Horizon History of Africa.* New York: American Heritage, 1971. An excellent anthology covering African history from its emergence to colonial rule.

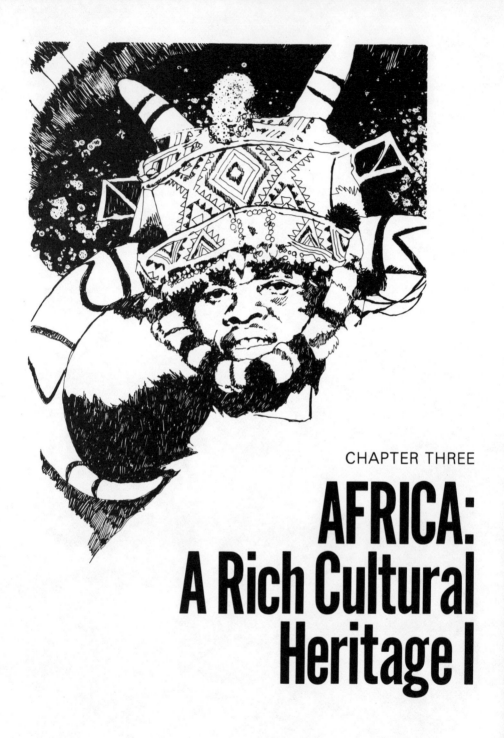

CHAPTER THREE

AFRICA: A Rich Cultural Heritage I

There is no wealth where there are no children.
(AFRICAN PROVERB)

OVERVIEW

To understand Africa's cultural heritage, one has to look at Africa's past and present political, economic, and social institutions. The past has served as the foundation for what exists today. Many institutions have changed while others have remained basically the same, and, in some instances, the old institutions and modified ones exist side by side.

This chapter examines historical, political, and social institutions and illustrates how they are part of contemporary African culture. In African societies there exists a wide variety of social and political institutions. Although there is tremendous diversity among these societies, there are key elements present in all. Lifestyles in African societies are influenced by each society's system of kinship and descent; by that society's beliefs about the transition from childhood to adulthood; and by that society's beliefs about justice.

A person's status in life and role in the community are determined most often by membership in a specific kinship and descent group. The kinship and descent group actually shapes the society's social and political institutions. Each society holds strong beliefs about bride prices, polygamy, relationships between husbands and wives, raising children, the position of children in society, and the governing power of elders.

In order for any society to be perpetuated, there must be a conscious effort to guide the youth into adulthood so that they can assume roles that guarantee the society's continued existence. The process through which African societies teach their young the adult roles and values ranges from having informal apprentice-type instruction in some societies to more formal manhood and womanhood training schools in other societies. In nearly all cases, however, this transition is a tense and conflict-ridden experience. There is some relief of this tension provided by contact with others who are undergoing similar experiences. Most societies have some organized pattern of age grouping. An "age-set" is composed of all persons (all ages, both sexes) who are initiated together. Other societies use "age-grades" as an indication of a person's state of development in the growing-up process. A person's age-grade may indicate his job in society—hunter, warrior, elder, and so forth. Age grouping or generational class frequently determines the ritual and political roles that a person assumes in the community.

OBJECTIVES

As a result of studying this chapter, you should be able to:
1. Describe kinship and descent in African social organization by comparing and contrasting child rearing in a matrilineal and patrilineal society.
2. Distinguish among the various units (family, clan, tribe) in African society by stating the role of each unit.

3. Analyze the impact of polygamy on the African family unit by charting a traditional extended family and labeling the social roles of each of its members.

4. Recognize the prime importance of African socialization processes by contrasting how youths become adults in any two African societies.

5. Assess the importance of ancestors and unborn children in African families by discussing how they influence the thoughts and behavior of living family members.

6. Describe the political hierarchy of Songhay by explaining the responsibilities of the king, the administrators, and the advisors.

7. Discuss the system of investiture by describing the role of the electing family and the enthroning family.

8. Identify the economic principles upon which African socialism is based by describing the western African concept of land ownership.

9. Discuss the specialization of labor in western African societies by describing the labor functions that characterized the precolonial period.

10. Describe the labor system used in precolonial western Africa by identifying the responsibilities of men, women, and children.

MAJOR THEMES
SOCIAL INSTITUTIONS: FAMILY

In traditional African societies, the family consisted of many members including children, parents, grandparents, uncles, aunts, etc. The concept of a nuclear family (mother, father, children) did not exist. In many societies there are "extended families." This could mean that two or more brothers established families in one area quite close to one another and live as one large family. Or it could mean, in polygamous societies, that a man and his several wives and their children lived in a compound as one large family.

Since most traditional African societies allow polygamy, family relationships that do not exist in monogamous societies are prevalent, especially the roles of co-wives and half-siblings. In successful polygamous marriages, there are separate houses for each wife or each group of wives; there is usually a separate dwelling for the husband. Each co-wife is responsible particularly for her own children, but also for the welfare of all the family members. Men are expected to treat their wives in keeping with their stations rather than equally. First wives usually hold the strongest position. It is the husband's job to keep all of them content and to make sure all the children are well fed and clothed. The number of wives a man may have varies from four in Muslim societies to any number he can readily afford in other societies.

African families also include departed relatives and unborn members. Surviving members are taught not to forget the dead. Deceased members of a family are always recalled in praise-singing and storytelling. Unborn members are regarded as a continuation of the family. Therefore, African parents look forward to the marriages of their sons and daughters, and particularly to the birth of grandchildren, as assuring the perpetuation of the family as a whole.

SOCIAL INSTITUTIONS: CLAN

Anthropologically, "clan" means a group of people who claim common descent. The common descent can be either from the male side (patrilineal) or the female (matrilineal) or both. If the clan is patrilineal, the major responsibility for raising children goes to the father and his family—the children belong to the father. If the common descent derives from the female side, the children are the responsibility of the mother and her family (usually the mother's brother), and the children belong to the mother's family. In clans that recognize both the female and the male side, the question of claiming the children is more complex.

There is a strong bond felt among clan members. It is usually attributed to having common descent, but it is fortified in other ways—possessing common land; living in a common area; and sharing a common totem (a protective, and therefore, sacred animal, plant, or other object). It is believed that all who have the same totem are to be treated as brothers because totems, just as last names, are passed from father to son. They indicate that a blood relationship exists between the totem and all members of the group which bear the totem name. Intermarriage between families of a common totem are rare. After several generations, representatives of the same totem group may quite likely be spread over a large area. But when one person meets another of the same totem, they consider themselves fellow members of one clan.

SOCIAL INSTITUTIONS: TRIBE

Much confusion exists about the definition of a tribe. For our purpose, "tribe" means "an agglomeration of groups and individuals, not necessarily related, (forming) a cultural and political community through living in a common territory, having a common leader, one language, and similar customs and usages". Some African tribes have been described as little more than village-states; still others, including thousands of people and thousands of square miles, have been described as empires. Others are described as language groups.

Traditionally, all tribal units, whether small or large, had a chief or paramount chief at its head. The chief was, and in many instances still is, the symbol of power. Principal functions of the chief were to administer law and to protect both tribal members and tribal heritage and customs. Chieftainship has always been instrumental in fostering political unity, shaping public opinion, directing community enterprise, and nurturing religious sentiment.

POLITICAL INSTITUTIONS

The political traditions of western African civilizations during the period from A.D. 800 through A.D. 1500 were initially based on the village community structure. The political organizations ranged from simple, isolated family states to highly organized federated kingdoms.

The power to govern the state resided in a specified royal family. The other families played a vital role in the political hierarchy. The electing family had the responsibility of designating the most capable member of the royal family as its leader when a vacancy occurred at the top of the political hierarchy. The selected member of the royal family did not have to be the first-born. The enthroning family had the responsibility of investing the new head of state into office. The new leader could not exercise any authority without first being enthroned by the enthroning family.

The political organization of Mali and Songhay was influenced by the Islamic faith, which became the state religion. The rulers of these empires improved the political administration of their governments by using principles of the Koran for administrative and judicial purposes.

ECONOMIC INSTITUTIONS

The primary economic orientation of western Africa was African socialism. Essentially, western Africans were agriculturally oriented. The land was so important to the general welfare of the community that collective ownership was a prevailing principle very early in economic development. This collective ownership was also applied to other productive areas of the economy.

The entire community was involved in harvesting, threshing, milling, and storing produce. The agricultural products were then equally distributed to all members of the village. Domestic animals were individually owned. In many instances, a man's wealth could be measured by the size of his cattle or goat herds. However, owners of cattle and goats were required to share the meat of their herds after slaughter. These early societies exhibited a high degree of specialization of labor.

The early economies of western Africa were stimulated by commercial ties with the Arab world. Islam played a vital economic role in the expanded trade relations between the Arab and western African worlds.

LEARNING ACTIVITIES

To accomplish the objectives of this chapter, you should do the following:
A. Study the chapter Overview.

B. Read the Major Themes.

C. Read Chapter Three in the anthology.

D. Examine carefully Section III of the Continuity Table.

E. Answer these questions.

1. What social units are you a part of that are similar in role and structure to social units in Africa?

2. What family roles exist in polygamous societies that do not exist in monogamous societies?

3. How do the feelings of African mothers and fathers toward their children compare to the feelings of American mothers and fathers toward their children?

4. How is the transition from childhood to adulthood accomplished in American society? Do Americans have socialization rituals that are comparable to those in various African societies?

5. How and why are ancestors and unborn children important in African societies?

6. What was African socialism? What comparisons can be made between African socialism and contemporary socialism?

POSTEVALUATION

To check your learning, select the most appropriate answer to each of the following questions:

1. In patrilineal societies
   a. the descent is traced through the female line.
   b. the mother's brother and father determine the patterns of authority and precedence.
   c. more status and precedence are given to elder members than to junior ones.
   d. all of the above.

2. The intense feeling of oneness or commonness that exists among the members of a clan in Africa is usually attributed to
   a. having common interests.
   b. having common descent.
   c. having common birthmarks.
   d. having common language.

3. Polygamous societies in Africa
   a. have familial relationships that parallel closely the familial relationships in monogamous societies.
   b. have benefits such as greater distribution of labor.
   c. are rarely affected by jealousy or envy because each wife and respective family is well cared for.
   d. are the result of a crucial shortage of women.

4. The political organizations among Africans were centralized and based on divine kinship. Nonetheless, the kings did not enjoy complete sovereignty because
   a. the power of the local kings was indisputable in matters of local concern.
   b. a division of authority kept the great kings sensitive to the possibility of conflict within their kingdom.
   c. military organizations kept a constant vigil on the operations of organized central government.
   d. all of the above.
   e. only (a) and (b) are correct.
5. According to the African concept of landownership
   a. the land belonged to the ruling family in the area.
   b. the land belonged to individuals.
   c. the land belonged to the first families to arrive in the area.
   d. the land belonged to the collective community.

(For correct answers, see ANSWER KEY.)

ANNOTATED BIBLIOGRAPHY

Davidson, Basil. *African Kingdom.* New York: Time Inc., 1966. A well-illustrated pictorial study of African kingdoms. This is also an easily read book that provides an accurate account of African civilizations south of the Sahara.

Franklin, John Hope. *From Slavery to Freedom.* New York: Knopf, 1961. This book was one of the early enlarged editions. The volume is well documented, well written, and very readable. It contains valuable information on the cradle of civilization that is not included in later editions.

Toppin, Edgar. *A Biographical History of Blacks in America: Since 1528.* New York: McKay, 1969. This book by Toppin provides the reader with historical materials that no other books provide. Toppin writes in a very personalized, scholarly style that readers will enjoy.

CHAPTER FOUR

AFRICA: A Rich Cultural Heritage II

Life is a mixture of joy and suffering and so we must learn to accept both, and the acceptance of both is a sign of maturity. (AFRICAN PROVERB)

OVERVIEW

Thus far the social and political structures that exist in Africa have been presented in an effort to show the richness of African culture. These two structures provide a somewhat historical picture. To update that picture and to show how dynamic African cultures always have been, and still are, one needs to consider other institutions and elements. Close examination of language, art, and religion will reflect not only the character of African peoples, but also their creativity.

Too often, the many languages of Africa have been mistakenly labeled as dialects, distortions, or patois. There are four major families of languages comprising several hundred separate and distinct languages, and most Africans speak several of these languages with ease.

African art, or at least aspects of it, has been studied for ages, but this art has been viewed mostly in terms of form rather than function, i.e., African art has been created in order to assist or implement some other activity or function in life—religion, magic, or fertility. African religions have over the centuries been the victims of gross misconceptions and myths.

This chapter will serve to clarify many mistaken ideas and thus help students to more fully appreciate African culture.

OBJECTIVES

As a result of studying this chapter, you should be able to:
1. Recognize that many languages exist in Africa by comparing the four major language families and the areas where they are spoken.
2. Differentiate among the different types of African sculpture by identifying the three categories into which African sculpture falls.
3. Recognize the complexity of African music by describing the role of poly-rhythms in its composition.
4. Differentiate among the various African musical instruments by putting them into categories.
5. Recognize the multifunctional aspects of African art by describing the relationship between art and life.
6. Validate that all traditional African religions are basically monotheistic by discussing the role of the Supreme God.
7. Recognize the role of rituals in African religions by listing events that are ritualized.
8. State the influence of traditional religions on Islam and Christianity by giving examples of how traditional beliefs modified original expressions of Islam and Christianity.

MAJOR THEMES
AFRICAN LANGUAGES

There are many African languages; estimates of the number of indigenous languages range from 800 to 1,500. African languages have been grouped by linguists into four major language families: *Khoisan,* the "'click" languages, spoken by the Bushmen and Hottentots and other people of southwestern Africa and Tanzania; *Niger-Congo,* spoken over most of Africa, south of the Dakar-Mombasa line; *Nilo-Saharan,* spoken from central Sudan to the Great Lakes region; and the *Afro-Asiatic,* which includes languages spoken in northeastern and northern Africa as well as the Semitic languages of southwestern Asia.

Pidgin is spoken as a second language in many western African coastal areas. It developed as a result of trading between Europeans and Africans. It is often used as a lingua franca (commercial or trade language) between neighboring villages with different languages and in cities between speakers who do not have a common language. It should be noted that many Africans speak several, perhaps four to six, languages.

In most African states, one will find many different languages indigenous to the area. In Nigeria alone, more than 200 languages (covering three of the language families) are spoken or used in the communications media. This language diversity is one of the most unique and challenging features in the development of Africa today.

AFRICAN ART

Probably the most important characteristic of African art is that it is multifunctional. Rarely has African artwork been done in the mold of "art for art's sake." Instead, most African art is related to other aspects of life and is closely associated with religion.

Sculpture is one of the main forms of African expression that is widely recognized. African sculpture falls into three categories: figurines, stools, and masks. Most African sculptors work either in green wood or alloys of copper, zinc, bronze, and brass.

Music is the other major facet of African art with a distinct quality. The most striking feature about African music is the use of polyrhythms. These are complex combinations of different rhythms all played at the same time. In African music anywhere from five to twelve different rhythms have been recorded. African instruments vary from drums and simple rattles to strings. In addition, the body acts as an instrument, with hand-clapping and foot-stomping.

Polyrhythmic music is the foundation for the complexity in African dance. Different parts of the body accompany different rhythms in the music. So the dancers' bodies reproduce the polyrhythms in the music—heads move to one beat, shoulders to another, arms to another, and so forth.

It should not be forgotten that music and dance are functional in African society. There is an interaction between the musical structure and its social purpose. Music and dance are ritualistic and ceremonial for certain events in life.

Other aspects of African art include proverbs, poetry, songs, storytelling, praise-singing, as well as drama, which capitalizes on the verbal and musical art expressions. All African art forms have served to reinforce, create, or perpetuate various traditions, history, ideals, structures, concerns, and values in African societies. All demonstrate a relationship between art and life.

AFRICAN RELIGION

Many misconceptions and myths exist concerning African religions. Practically all African religions acknowledge a supreme God, but not necessarily the same one. This high God, in any of these denominations, is perceived as the creator of the world, including mankind, and as the major source of orderliness. In this respect, all major African religions are monotheistic. Some of them, however, practice polytheism by believing in not only a supreme God, but several lesser gods, spirits, ancestors, or other divinities. These lesser dieties are construed as intermediaries between man and the high God.

Another generality that can be made is that African religions are tribal religions. They have a direct association with a tribe or social group, and thus they are not international or global. A religion suitable for one tribe may be quite inappropriate for another, because much of the religion is shaped by ancestry, and the ancestry of each tribe is different.

Prayers, sacrifices, and other rituals play a chief role in the practice of African religions. Prayers and sacrifices are used as channels of communication between man and divinity. The purpose of rituals is multifold. Religious rituals, the nature of which is determined by the tribe or religion, mark each event that occurs in life.

Although tribal religions are prevalent, they have been threatened by Islam and Christianity. These two major faiths have opposed tribal beliefs as well as each other for centuries. A fair portion of Africa is Christian. The Coptic Church, found in Ethiopia and Egypt, is one of the basic forms of Christianity. In northeastern Africa, Christianity lost out to Islam, which has spread widely across the Sudanic lands and down the eastern coast of the continent. Many African countries refer to themselves as Christian or Muslim nations.

LEARNING ACTIVITIES

To accomplish the objectives of this chapter, you should do the following:
A. Study the chapter Overview.
B. Read the Major Themes.

C. Read Chapter Four in the anthology.
D. Examine carefully Section IV of the Continuity Table.
E. Answer these questions.
  1. How can the existence of so many languages be problematic? What solutions can you offer?
  2. How has African art influenced Western artists? What were the functions of each type of African sculpture?
  3. How does the occurrence of polyrhythms in African music affect African dance? How does African dancing differ from Western ballroom dancing?
  4. How are the construction of African instruments representative of the land and culture where they are found? What various uses are there in African society for the drum?
  5. How is African art multifunctional? What relationships exist between various art forms and other aspects of life?
  6. How can a society be both monotheistic and polytheistic at the same time?
  7. What are the major rituals in African religions? What events in life and nature are ritualized in African religions?
  8. What impact have Islam and Christianity had on African history? What impact have they on African culture today?
  9. How have traditional religious beliefs been modified by contact with Islam and Christianity?
F. (Optional) Answer these questions based on the *Roots* story.
  1. What were the different languages spoken in Juffure and the surrounding villages?
  2. Which utensils, tools, or other items used in the daily life of the Mandinga are examples of functional African art?
  3. What specific uses were made of the drums?

POSTEVALUATION

To check your learning, select the most appropriate answer to each of the following questions:

1. Which of the following is not correct? The four major African language families and the areas where they are spoken are
  a. Khoisan, spoken by the peoples in southwestern Africa and Tanzania.
  b. Niger-Congo, spoken over most of Africa south of the Kalahari Desert.
  c. Nilo-Saharan, spoken from central Sudan to the Great Lakes region.
  d. Afro-Asiatic, spoken in northeastern and northern Africa.
2. African music has been described as complex. It differs from Western music because it
  a. is based on a different tonal scale.
  b. consists of several polyrhythms.

   c. consists of a major theme and variations of the theme.
   d. has an accelerated tempo.
3. African art is rarely done for esthetics alone. Instead it is
   a. considered to be art for art's sake.
   b. meant to draw a distinction between man and God.
   c. simply another religious ritual.
   d. functional in African societies.
4. Traditional religions have constantly fought against and often lost out to
   a. Islam and Christianity.
   b. Buddhism and Christianity.
   c. Islam and Buddhism.
   d. all three religions mentioned above.
5. Much credit for recording African history must go to the *griots* for
   a. praise-singing and storytelling.
   b. African theater.
   c. dance rituals.
   d. poetry and songs.
(For correct answers, see ANSWER KEY.)

ANNOTATED BIBLIOGRAPHY

Bohannon, Paul. *Africa and Africans.* New York: The Natural History Press, 1964. This easily read book has a detailed section on traditional African cultures. Chapters on language, religion, and art show the degree of complexity in African cultures and appropriately warn against overgeneralizing.

Clark, Leon E. (ed.). *Through African Eyes: Cultures in Change.* New York: Praeger, 1970. This anthology is a unique approach to the study of Africa which offers lively firsthand stories of African life and culture. Most of the accounts are written by Africans.

Davidson, Basil. *The African Genius.* Boston: Little, Brown, 1969. This book is an excellent empirical introduction to the study of Africa's cultural and social history.

CHAPTER FIVE

AFRICA TO AMERICA: The Beginnings of Slavery

The goat says, "What will come has already come."
(AFRICAN PROVERB)

OVERVIEW

African culture reached out to touch the lives of other people in other places as blacks from Africa participated in voyages around the world. While previous chapters examined African history and African culture as it exists or existed on the African continent, this chapter will examine the diffusion of African culture. Black Africans played a role in the European exploration of the New World from the beginning. They accompanied Columbus, were with Balboa when he viewed the calm of the Pacific Ocean, and with Cortes when he conquered Mexico.

Some evidence indicates that black contact with the indigenous populations of the Americas may have occurred as early as 1200 to 650 B.C. Mexican scientists have found evidence of an intermingling of African blood with that of the Lacondones, a highly isolated people in a remote area, based on the identification of the sickle-cell gene, a gene unique to the black race. Additional evidence is suggested by the magnificent carved stone colossi of the Olmec era, a discovery that startled the world both because of their size and their Negroid facial characteristics. Theories of early African-American contact are not uniformly accepted. Skeptical scholars suggest that the Negroid features of the colossi are mere accidents, claiming that such contacts were highly improbable because of the navigational difficulties in crossing the Atlantic, and because it was unlikely that ancient sailing vessels could make such a voyage. Such arguments have been in part refuted by the voyage of the Ra, a similar vessel that made the trans-Atlantic crossing successfully.

This chapter examines the presence of African blacks in the New World. It considers the social and political situations in Africa that allowed blacks to leave or be taken from African shores for the pursuit of European interests that ultimately formed the basis of the exploitation of African blacks. Finally, this segment briefly explores the comparative approach to the study of slavery in diverse geographical areas.

OBJECTIVES

As a result of studying this chapter, you should be able to:
1. Validate pre-Columbian African presence in the Americas by describing the evidence that supports their presence.
2. Discuss the treatment of slaves captured in Africa by describing the conditions they had to endure.
3. Describe the middle passage by comparing its impact upon slaves and crew.
4. Recognize Portuguese economic interests in Africa by identifying three motives for Prince Henry's organized voyages.
5. Discuss the importance of sugar to the development of slavery by describing the role of slavery in sugar production.

6. Discuss the merit of the comparative approach to the study of slavery by identifying the advantages of this method.
7. Define Mediterranean bondage by describing three of its characteristics.
8. Identify Alfonso I's dissatisfaction with the Portuguese by describing the nature of his protest letters.

MAJOR THEMES
PRE-COLUMBIAN PRESENCE

The presence of Old World cotton in the Americas is viewed by some as proof of pre-Columbian contacts with the New World. Research suggests that all Old World cotton, wild or domesticated, has 13 large chromosomes. There is a major difference between this and the New World variety. Wild cotton in the New World has 13 chromosomes, but cultivated cotton has 26—13 large and 13 small. In the wild species of American cotton there are no large chromosomes. The fact that cultivated cotton in the New World has 13 large chromosomes suggests that some Old World contact was necessary. How then did the Old World cotton arrive in the Americas? Obviously, the methods of transport were very limited; either plants or seeds floated safely across the Atlantic, or they were carried on ancient voyages. The latter position, which should be given attention, argues for the introduction of Old World cotton and the methods of cultivation by those accustomed to its use. The question of pre-Columbian contacts is not yet a closed issue. This and other evidence, such as the blood factor discussed earlier, suggests the possibility of the presence of Africans and other Old World peoples in the Americas before Columbus.

SLAVERY

The institution of slavery, as it developed in the New World, had its origins in Europe where, at the end of the medieval period, Europeans were laying the foundations of New World slavery. As they established businesses in the eastern portion of the Mediterranean basin, it was found that sugar could be successfully grown on the island of Cyprus and exported to Europe for a profit. It grew so well that the plantation owners were faced with a labor shortage. White slaves, captured in the Levantine wars, were imported to do the hard work. They were chattel; they worked in gangs; they were kept separate from the rest of society and had no social mobility.

Meanwhile, news reached Europe of a New World with thousands of acres of virgin land. When Constantinople fell to the Turks in 1453, the source of white slaves had been cut off. The basis for the trans-Atlantic slave trade was established, once it was realized that slaves could be obtained from black Africa and that sugar grew well in the New World.

Portugal was the first of the modern European powers to make contact with West Africa.

Prince Henry, known as "the Navigator," organized exploratory voyages to enhance the wealth and military strength of his kingdom. Henry felt that such voyages would provide a new route to the East, spread the Christian faith to pagans, and secure new allies against the Arabs. At the time of his death in 1460, Portugal was enjoying great economic returns from Africa.

The economic success of Portugal left ruin and misery in Africa. During the rule of the Christian king Mbemba Nzinga, renamed Alfonso I, the Portuguese plundered Kongo-Angola and enslaved many people. Alfonso wrote numerous letters to the Portuguese government expressing his concern for his people and his dissatisfaction with the Portuguese colonists. The Portuguese exploitation typified the behavior of other European colonists in Africa as the demand for slaves reached its zenith in the seventeenth and eighteenth centuries.

After Christopher Columbus' voyage to the New World in 1492, Spain quickly claimed the lands of the New World. As Spanish conquistadores destroyed the indigenous civilization of the Americas, they forced Indians into slave labor. The Indians, unaccustomed to this kind of harsh labor, soon began to die.

With the discovery of gold in Latin America, the demand for slaves increased. By this time, the coast of West Africa was dotted with various European colonial outposts. Though Spain and Portugal had dominated the slave trade for over a century, other European nations began to recognize the profits and got involved. The Dutch came in the sixteenth century; the English in the seventeenth century. Early in the eighteenth century the English seized control of the slave trade from the Dutch and established England as the mistress of the seas.

Africans were procured as slaves in various ways. Some were captured by Europeans; others were captured by Africans and sold or traded to Europeans in exchange for cheap textiles, iron products, guns, and spirits.

Large, powerful African kingdoms made war upon small nations for the purpose of taking slaves. These captives faced harsh conditions. Many of the people were captured in the interior, chained, and forced to make the long march to the sea. As they arrived at the sea, starved and frightened, the old and the sick were separated from the healthy. The slaves were then branded and housed in barracoons until they were ready to be shipped to the New World. Seeing the opportunity to cash in on the demand for slaves, the African ruling elite class was just as responsible as the Europeans for the pain and terror created in West Africa.

Before the African slave could stand on the soil of the Americas, he would have to undergo the ordeal of the "middle passage," which was the Atlantic crossing. For the Africans this was a living hell: they were cramped into the hold of a ship and chained; the heat was stifling; the food was rotten; disease was rampant aboard ship; and medical care was, at best, poor.

The terror experienced by slaves during the middle passage is brought to stark reality by Haley's description in *Roots*—the raking of naked slave backs against rough, vibrating planks; fear tightening and swelling chests almost to the point of bursting; the pounding of blood in heads that could not comprehend what was happening; terror, like a wild animal, clawing and tearing at the vital organs; men thrashing and lunging against shackles; the inescapable bedlam of rattling chains; men screaming in prayer and smashing their heads and bodies against planking. The mind probably cannot truly comprehend such conditions—conditions that resulted in the death of many Africans from "fixed melancholy" (extreme depression) and from suicide.

It should be remembered, however, that the crews of these ships also endured the rotten food, the disease, and the lack of medical care. The ships' captains, strongly aware of profits involved, often worked to keep the human cargo healthy. The whites aboard were of no economic value. Crews were, therefore, often brutally treated, faring as badly as the slaves, or worse.

Once the ships docked in the West Indies, the African was faced with the auction block. Every part of his anatomy was examined by prospective buyers.

John Newton

"Amazing Grace," an old favored hymn sung often in black American churches, was written by John Newton, a one-time slave dealer and slave ship captain. It is ironic that a man with such a past should write such a hymn, but his life was one of irony.

He was converted to Christianity while passing time reading Thomas Kempis' *Imitation of Christ* and experiencing harsh ship conditions filled with life-saving miracles. He left slave trading and became a preacher with a large following. Common people were attracted to this "rebel," who did unheard of things in church; i.e., having devotional service, Bible meetings, church school, and using hymns instead of singing psalms. Many of these hymns he wrote, and with help he published them in *The Olney Hymns*. Included in this collection was "Amazing Grace." The song itself is Newton's testimony, as is his tombstone epitaph, which tells the story of his life from bad boy to "messenger of the Lord." (From Albert Edward Bailey, *The Gospel in Hymns*, New York, Scribner's, 1950, p. 127.)

JOHN NEWTON
CLERK
ONCE AN INFIDEL AND LIBERTINE
A SERVANT OF SLAVES IN AFRICA
WAS
BY THE RICH MERCY OF OUR LORD AND SAVIOUR
JESUS CHRIST
PRESERVED, RESTORED, PARDONED
AND APPOINTED TO PREACH THE FAITH
HE HAD LONG LABORED TO DESTROY.

When the sale was completed, he was taken to the plantation where he embarked upon the "seasoning" period; that is, the period during which he became acquainted with his new environment. Life on plantations was hard, and many slaves were literally worked to death. Some West Indian planters believed that it was cheaper to buy more slaves than to provide proper care and moderate working hours for them.

In North America, in 1619, a new drama began to unfold. The transplanting of African people to American soil was the beginning of the saga of American slavery. Before we examine that drama, we must turn our attention briefly to a comparative examination of slavery in the Americas.

COMPARATIVE APPROACH

Many historians now believe that the study of American slavery should not be studied in isolation; that the comparative method should be used to enhance our understanding of slavery in general and the uniqueness of United States slavery in particular. For instance, the word "treatment" should be used and interpreted with extreme care. This word has been construed in several different ways by scholars: the day-to-day care of slaves (food, clothing, shelter); the means by which slaves gained manumission; and the existence of provisions for the development of strong family ties and sound personalities.

Some scholars argue that slaves were treated more humanely in the Portuguese and Spanish colonies than in the colonies dominated by Anglo-Saxons. In Latin America, the Church, the Crown, and the feudal economy provided an atmosphere that was more responsive to the slave as a person than was true in the English colonies. The Catholic Church sought to save the souls of the slaves. The Crown made sure that slave abuses were held in check, thereby ensuring protection of their investments. The feudal economy of Latin America made room for the training of slaves in a wide variety of skills (the Portuguese and Spanish planters had a certain disdain for physical labor, as opposed to their northern counterparts).

In Anglo-America, there was no royal influence to protect the rights of slaves, no organized Church effort to fight for the salvation of slaves, and the crude system that developed in Anglo-America considered the slave as a chattel. In fact, there was a large, white, indentured class that restricted the variety of job-training opportunities available to slaves.

Manumissions were granted with greater frequency in Brazil and Cuba than in the English colonies, though many were granted for reasons of economic expediency rather than for reasons of humanity. Nevertheless, the planter class in the United States was not receptive to the idea of granting slaves their freedom. They feared having a large, free, black population because such a group would constitute a threat to the institution of slavery. Throughout the South, when

manumissions occurred, ex-slaves were ordered to leave the vicinity or be reenslaved. By the time slavery was abolished in Brazil (1888), most slaves there were
already free. In Anglo-America, blackness tended to become synonymous with
slavery, which greatly restricted the social mobility of blacks. In Latin America,
the idea that "money whitens" was more pervasive and therefore allowed for a
greater social mobility of blacks.

Contrary to this viewpoint, recent comparative studies of Latin American
slavery and North American slavery revealed that the Latin system was as harsh
as that of the Anglo institution. Many abuses have been noted in the Brazilian
system: the freeing of old and crippled slaves; the use of slave women as prosti-
tutes; the poor hygiene of the slave quarters; and the use of tin masks to prevent
consumption of liquor and dirt. One crucial difference between the two systems
seems to have been the attitude toward the mulatto in Latin America. Where no
"mulatto escape hatch" developed in the United States, the concept of race was
blurred in Cuba and Brazil. The mulatto was neither black nor white, while in
North America only black and white were recognized. Thus, the mulatto escape
hatch available to those of mixed blood in Latin America allowed them to be
absorbed into the wider society and, at the same time, helped to close the social
gap between the races.

LEARNING ACTIVITIES

To accomplish the objectives of this chapter, you should do the following:
A. Study the chapter Overview.
B. Read the Major Themes.
C. Read Chapter Five in the anthology.
D. Examine carefully Section V of the Continuity Table.
E. Answer these questions.
   1. How does New World cotton lend support for pre-Columbian presence
      in the New World?
   2. Since there was no standard African currency, what means were used to
      purchase slaves?
   3. What differences existed between Latin America and North America in
      the practice of slavery?
   4. What motives prompted exploration and colonization in both Africa and
      the New World?
   5. Why did Africans sell their own people into bondage?
   6. How did sugar affect the development of slavery in West Africa and in
      the New World?
   7. Do you think the trauma of the middle passage could have been made less
      severe for the Africans?

8. Were there powerful means at the disposal of the African kings to prevent European colonization?

POSTEVALUATION

To check your learning, select the most appropriate answer to each of the following questions:

1. The first modern European nation to make contact with West Africa was
   a. Italy.
   b. Portugal.
   c. France.
   d. Spain.
2. The development of slavery in the Americas was based on the fact
   a. that conditions were conducive to sugar cultivation.
   b. that Indians had cultivated sugar there for centuries.
   c. that sugar required less attention than the cultivation of other staples.
   d. that black Africans had experience in sugar cultivation.
3. The standard currency used to buy slaves in Africa was
   a. gold.
   b. guns.
   c. rum.
   d. none of the above.
4. Africans suffered from "fixed melancholy" because
   a. living conditions aboard the slave ships were inhumane.
   b. they felt they would never return to their homeland.
   c. they lost the will to live.
   d. all of the above.
5. The colossi offer evidence of the African presence in America because
   a. they are made with a special West African gold.
   b. the facial features of the stone heads have Negroid characteristics.
   c. the primitive Indians had no artistic skills.
   d. Columbus indicated in his records that most of the Indians had Negroid features.

(For correct answers, see ANSWER KEY.)

ANNOTATED BIBLIOGRAPHY

The following works give a rather complete history of the development of slavery in Africa; the beginnings of the slave trade; the demographic settlements of slaves; the impact of slavery upon Africa; and the economic aspects of the slave trade:

Ajayi, Ade, F. J., and Ian Espie (ed.). *A Thousand Years of West African History.* Ibadan,

Nigeria: Ibadan University Press, 1965. An excellent anthology on West African history that deals with the empires, slave trade, nationalism, colonial rule, and independence.

Bennett, Norman R. *Africa and Europe: From Roman Times to the Present.* New York: Africana, 1975. Bennett explores the nature of contacts between Africa and Europe from ancient times to the present. It is an excellent introductory text for the beginning student's encounter with Africa.

Curtin, Philip D. *The Atlantic Slave Trade: A Census.* Madison: University of Wisconsin Press, 1969.

Davidson, Basil. *Black Mother: The Years of the Trade.* Boston: Atlantic Monthly Press, 1961.

Degler, Carl. *Neither Black nor White: Slavery and Race Relations in Brazil.* New York: Macmillan, 1971. This authoritative source advances the thesis that Latin American slavery was just as harsh as was the North American system. The author argues that the major difference between the two systems was found in the status accorded the mulatto.

Donnan, Elizabeth (ed.). *Documents Illustrative of the History of Slave Trade to America,* 4 vols. New York: Octagon, 1965. The primary sources of information contained in these four volumes are excellent. One scholar has suggested that the massive and complete information in Donnan's volumes contains many books not yet written.

Duffy, James. *Portuguese Africa.* Cambridge, Mass.: Harvard University Press, 1961. This book is a detailed account of the first modern European nation that made contact with West Africa. Duffy covers the intrusion of the Portuguese into Africa from the 1440s to the late 1950s.

Fisher, Allan G. B., and Humphrey J. Fisher. *Slavery and Muslim Society in Africa: The Institution in Saharan and Sudanic Africa and the Trans-Saharan Trade.* Garden City, N.Y.: Doubleday Anchor Books, 1972. A complete analysis of domestic slavery and the participation of the Muslims in that trade. Although much of the information deals with the nineteenth century, it offers insight into the historical development of the Arab-controlled slave trade.

Mannix, Daniel P., and Malcolm Cowley. *Black Cargoes: A History of the Atlantic Slave Trade.* New York: Viking, 1962.

CHAPTER SIX

SLAVERY:
The Birth of the
Industrial Revolution

What cannot be helped, must be endured.
(AFRICAN PROVERB)

OVERVIEW

Slavery was a profitable business. Although involvement did not guarantee riches, great fortunes were amassed by many individuals. The profits from the slave trade contributed to the accumulation of capital required to finance the Industrial Revolution that transformed the United States and the nations of Europe into modern industrialized societies. The Industrial Revolution carried with it both positive and negative results. Although there were many advances in industry, agriculture, and medicine and many more new job opportunities, the revolution also brought new kinds of poverty, misery, and disillusionment. Thousands of men, women, and children became urban dwellers, forced to live in congested slums and work under unsafe conditions.

Two factors requisite to the success of the Industrial Revolution, which began in Britain, were sufficient population and natural resources. The population explosion in Great Britain during the eighteenth century provided a population base large enough to support agricultural pursuits and to staff the expanding industrial system. Britain was also blessed with an abundance of natural resources (coal, iron, rivers). Coal and iron were the chief materials necessary to feed the expanding industries of all nations experiencing industrialization.

In this chapter, the industries that helped finance the Industrial Revolution will be highlighted. At the same time, the connection between slavery and the triangular trade will be explored. Finally, the impact on Africa of slavery and the Industrial Revolution is assessed.

OBJECTIVES

As a result of studying this chapter, you should be able to:
1. Discuss the implications of industrialization by describing the changes that occur in a society that undergoes the process.
2. Determine the relationship that existed between the slave trade and the Industrial Revolution by describing the contributions of slavery to the success of the revolution.
3. Discuss the negative impact of the Industrial Revolution by identifying hardships that resulted from it in Europe, America, and Africa.
4. Determine the effect of the slave trade on Africa's development during the Industrial Revolution by contrasting the economic growth of Europe with that of Africa during this period.
5. Explain the concept of "the triangular trade" by identifying each leg of the triangle as well as the goods traded.
6. Identify those nations that benefited most from the triangular trade by comparing the profits gained by each nation involved.

7. Point to the multiple profits made on each commodity exchanged in the triangular trade by explaining the eventual use of each commodity.

MAJOR THEMES
INDUSTRIAL ORDER

During the mid-eighteenth century Great Britain was the center of an industrial revolution that spread throughout western Europe and later to the United States. An industrialized nation is not simply a country of mechanized industrial activity but one in which the whole of society tends to become organized around machine technology. This process breaks down old values and replaces them with values that support the growth and expansion of industry and the reorganization of society in general.

The Industrial Revolution began in England with technological advances in the textile industry. For example, the flying shuttle enabled weavers to make wider cloth faster. The spinning jenny produced 8 threads at once. Such inventions did not come about as a result of a concerted scientific or governmental effort but because various individuals wanted progress. By applying these inventions to natural resources and accumulating sufficient capital from the triangular trade, Britain was able to launch a transformation of society previously unknown in world history.

By the 1820s the United States was on the brink of a miniature industrial revolution. Prior to that time, the steamboat had improved transportation, and the cotton gin, by speeding up the processing of cotton, had enlarged the export potential of that product and increased the need for slave labor. The westward movement of the nation, the building of roads, the development of canals, and the flowering of the banking system also helped propel America toward industrialization. The greatest industrial growth in the United States did not occur, however, until later in the nineteenth century.

AFRICAN CONTRIBUTIONS TO THE INDUSTRIAL ORDER

The contributions of Africa to the success of the industrial order should be examined thoughtfully. The agrarian economy of the southern colonies, later the southern states, was dependent upon a cheap labor pool that could withstand the rigors of the climate—and the African slave met this need. The Americas also provided a new outlet for European manufactured goods. African slaves cultivated cotton, sugar, indigo, and tobacco, which provided the raw materials for European factories. The income realized from agriculture was then used to buy finished goods. Tragically, the African slaves' contribution did not bring with it the concomitant industrial development of Africa.

TRIANGULAR TRADE

The wealth from the triangular trade helped establish the grandeur of the British Empire and aided in financing the Industrial Revolution. The trade route from England to Africa and then to the West Indies (plus mainland America) and back to England formed a perfect triangle. This trade, international in scope, contributed substantially to the tremendous growth of the economies of the western European nations during the second half of the eighteenth century.

Ships left England with cargos of manufactured goods to be exchanged in Africa for slaves. This human cargo, and other goods as well, were left in the West Indies and the United States. Reloaded with colonial and West Indian commodities, the ships returned to Great Britain. In essence, England provided the manufactured exports and the ships; Africa, the slave labor; and the colonies of the mainland and the West Indies, the raw materials. At each point of the exchange a profit was made, but England received the lion's share.

The sugar that was produced in abundance in the West Indies stimulated great wealth there and provided new jobs in sugar refining in England. When distilled, molasses, a by-product of sugar, produces rum. No ship left England without this important item; in fact, rum was lavishly supplied to chiefs and slave dealers to obtain a profitable load of human cargo. Although rum was not so crucial to the expanding economy of Great Britain as sugar, it produced great wealth for the West Indian economy. At the same time, wool, which had been important to the triangular trade in the early days, was later supplanted by cotton, revolutionizing the textile industry and providing thousands of jobs for British factory workers. Cotton cloth of many colors and prints was exported to Africa, thus increasing European industrial output through expanded trade.

The triangular trade had an impact on other sectors of society. Insurance agencies and banking underwent development and expansion. Shipbuilding, which experienced unparalleled growth, employed thousands of carpenters, sailors, and common laborers. Such growth led to the development of seaport centers like Bristol, Liverpool, and Glasgow. On the American mainland, the colonists were active participants in trade. In particular, the New England shipbuilding industry experienced tremendous development; ships carried food, horses, lumber, and other articles to the West Indies. This complex system of trade—an integral part of which was the slave business—provided profits as high as 200 percent to a wide variety of people including, strangely enough, Puritans and other religious groups. Since the colonies were a part of the British empire, they shared in the profits of the triangular trade, but not to the extent that Great Britain did.

AFRICA AND THE INDUSTRIAL REVOLUTION

As has been noted, the slave trade was an enormously profitable venture. Africa, however, did not share in the growth of industry and technology and the development of new towns. These were benefits evident in European nations and the Americas, but they were won at great cost to the cheap labor pool in each place. The cheapest of all was African slave labor. In fact, the goods taken to Africa by slave traders were of no enduring value to Africans and served primarily to stimulate the growth of factories and employment opportunities for Europeans.

The heavy demands that European industrialization placed upon Africa left indelible scars. It has been estimated that between 20 and 40 million Africans were taken across the Atlantic during the three centuries of the slave trade. Such loss of population destroyed entire villages. The insatiable demand for slaves promoted endless ethnic conflicts in Africa. Some nations completely disintegrated because of the slave trade, while others grew powerful by cooperation with slave traders. The individuals benefiting most from European contacts were the ruling elites of various African nations.

Although some scholars argue that the slave trade had little impact on African society, the losses suffered seem to refute this thesis. In Europe transportation and communication improved, economies grew, and the food supply increased, while in Africa internal development was at a standstill. Although Europe and Africa were entangled in a web of economic arrangements via the triangular trade, Africa experienced no industrial revolution. The practice of slavery was certainly a contributing factor to the successful industrialization of a number of nations. The costs, with virtually none of the benefits, were assessed against a key point of the triangle—Africa.

LEARNING ACTIVITIES

To accomplish the objectives of this chapter, you should do the following:
A. Study the chapter Overview.
B. Read the Major Themes.
C. Read Chapter Six in the anthology.
D. Examine carefully Section VI of the Continuity Table.
E. Answer these questions.
   1. How important was slavery to the Industrial Revolution?
   2. Were the poor living conditions produced by the Industrial Revolution inevitable?
   3. Why did Africa receive practically no benefits from the Industrial Revolution?

4. The Puritans were highly religious, yet they entered the business of the slave trade. Do you think that economic values tend to be more powerful motivators than religious values in everyday life?
5. Did Africa receive any enduring benefits from the slave trade?
6. Has technology produced more misery and problems than "progress"?
7. Was slavery necessary for the development of the Industrial Revolution?
8. How has your understanding of the importance of slavery to the growth of America increased?

POSTEVALUATION

To check your learning, select the most appropriate answer to each of the following questions:
1. The effect of the Industrial Revolution on Great Britain was that it produced
   a. a total reorganization of society around machines and technology.
   b. many new jobs for thousands of men, women, and children in factories.
   c. harsh living conditions for the many people living in newly formed slums.
   d. great wealth for many British capitalists.
   e. all of the above.
2. Technology can aid in the reorganization of society because it can
   a. break down old values and replace them with new ones.
   b. frighten people who are opposed to change.
   c. ensure an easier life for the people involved.
   d. bring progress and most people want progress.
3. The African continent is called "black mother" because
   a. all Africans have a dark complexion.
   b. Africa is the birthplace of humankind.
   c. the factory workers of Britain and France wanted to honor the continent.
   d. the planter class of the West Indies respected their black female house servants.
   e. none of the above.
4. The Industrial Revolution first began in
   a. France.
   b. England.
   c. the United States.
   d. Germany.
5. Major inventions of the Industrial Revolution were produced by
   a. governmental efforts.
   b. the Society of Scientists for Industrial Improvement.
   c. individual efforts.
   d. none of the above.

(For correct answers, see ANSWER KEY.)

ANNOTATED BIBLIOGRAPHY

Conrad, Alfred H., and John R. Meyer. *The Economics of Slavery and Other Studies in Econometric History.* Chicago: Aldine, 1964. A highly technical work that gives brilliant insights into British and American economic history through statistical analysis. One of the important points the book makes is the profitability of slavery to the southern economy.

Huberman, Leo. *Man's Worldly Goods: The Story of the Wealth of Nations.* New York: Monthly Review Press, 1961. This work traces the historical emergence of capitalism from feudalism. Huberman gives some attention to the importance of slavery in the rise of capitalism.

Oliver, Roland (ed.). *The Middle Age of African History.* London: Oxford University Press, 1967. A wide range of topics is included in this anthology; however, special attention should be given to Chapter 6, which analyzes the impact of the slave trade on traditional African society.

Rodney, Walter. *How Europe Underdeveloped Africa.* Dar es Salaam, Tanzania: Tanzania Publishing House, 1972. Rodney's thesis is simple: Africa's natural resources and its people aided the growth and expansion of Europe, but Africa's benefits from Europe were meager.

Williams, Eric. *Capitalism and Slavery.* Chapel Hill: The University of North Carolina Press, 1944. A must for any student who wants to understand the rise of the Industrial Revolution and the crucial role that slavery played.

CHAPTER SEVEN

SLAVERY:
Its Development
in Colonial America

If you sow falsehood, you reap deceit. (AFRICAN PROVERB)

OVERVIEW

The first white colonists in America were either adventurous gentlemen or persons from the lower levels of the English political and socioeconomic structure who had signed over their services for a period of time. This second group received the barest of life's necessities during the period of their indentured contracts. Indentured whites failed to resolve the chronic labor shortage in the colonies because of the limited term of their servitude and their retention of traditional English rights.

New historical evidence has invalidated many of the misconceptions concerning the period when blacks first reached colonial North America and their status upon arrival. Research suggests that the first blacks were taken to St. Augustine, Florida, on September 8, 1565, by the Spaniard, Pedro Menendez de Aviles. Twenty blacks were also taken to the colony of Jamestown, Virginia, in August 1619, probably as indentured servants.

White colonial attitudes concerning blacks appear to have been shaped before any physical contact occurred between the English and African peoples. Evidence seems to indicate that the English equated blackness with inferiority.

This chapter analyzes the political and socioeconomic status of white and black indentured servants. The chapter also describes the events that precipitated a change in the status of blacks from indentured servants to slaves for life.

OBJECTIVES

As a result of studying this chapter, you should be able to:
1. Analyze the political and socioeconomic status of white indentured servants by citing their rights as prescribed by English law.
2. Determine the relative status of black and white indentureds by describing the rights and privileges of each.
3. Describe the life styles of white indentured servants by analyzing their socioeconomic backgrounds and discussing their adjustments to servitude in the early colonial period.
4. Identify the principal cause for the onset of black de jure slavery by delineating the rationale used by white colonists.
5. Discuss the transition of blacks from indentured servants to slaves for life by describing the trends that illustrate it.
6. Differentiate between black indentured servants and slaves by examining Virginia's statutory designations to determine the status for each.
7. Describe the life style of black indentured servants by examining their early existence in North Hampton, Virginia.
8. Determine the impact that the African's color had upon the English by examining some of the early English attitudes about blackness.

9. Define the concept of racism by listing the genetic rationalizations that were developed and used to oppress people of African descent.
10. Discuss the reasons why colonists believed in black inferiority by analyzing white racial attitudes before the sixteenth century.

MAJOR THEMES

THE POLITICAL RIGHTS OF WHITE INDENTURED SERVANTS

The first Virginia colony was founded in 1607 along the James River. The colonists, who were gentlemen and laborers, encountered serious difficulties. They experienced much suffering from the moment they landed and began to build settlements at Jamestown. The basis of Virginia's future prosperity was laid with John Rolfe's successful experiment in growing and curing tobacco. The economy of Virginia grew with the demand for tobacco by Europeans, creating a labor shortage that could not be remedied by using local Indian labor.

The London and Virginia companies began to send poor, lower-class English whites to the colonies as indentured servants. Some of these people were from the slums of London and Liverpool. Many of them were taken from European debtors' prisons. A few of the indentured servants were also respectable whites who entered into indenture contracts with ship captains for passage to the colonies of America. Once in North America the indentured whites were considered to be servants of the master during their prescribed period of service. The American colonists used the word "servant" to describe all individuals who were not officers of the company.

The white indentured servant received the barest necessities for survival while under contract. Eventually, the supply of white indentured servants proved insufficient to satisfy increasing colonial labor demands, because according to English law, white servants could be indentured for only a short period before being released from service. Upon completion of the indentured contract, whites established themselves on farms and in businesses of their own. The stigma of past indentureship often made it difficult for the white freedman to achieve status and mobility in colonial Virginia.

THE INDENTURED STATUS OF BLACKS IN VIRGINIA AND MARYLAND

The first blacks who were taken to Jamestown bore Spanish names, were baptized, and appeared to have been assigned the same status as white indentured servants. The twenty Africans who were sold at Jamestown were captured either from a Spanish plantation or a Spanish ship by a Dutch privateer who exchanged them for supplies. These Africans had been converted to Christianity by their previous captors, the Spanish. Christian Africans from Spanish and Portuguese colonies in the Caribbean were able to secure indentured status in the English colonies if they could prove that they had been converted to Christianity.

Africans in the southern colonies could anticipate emancipation upon the completion of their terms of service. Some became free landowners in an economy in which tobacco became a very important cash crop. Prior to 1640, little is known historically about the treatment of indentured and free blacks.

> In 1624 William Tuchely, the son of Pedro and Isabella, was the first black child born in the colony of Virginia.

In the Virginia census enumerations of 1623–1624, blacks were listed as servants. Anthony Johnson's life is typical of the lives of indentured blacks who became free. Johnson reached Jamestown, Virginia, in 1621 as an indentured servant but became a free man and landowner upon completion of his term of service. He married a black and settled on 250 acres of land along the Pungoteague River in North Hampton County. Other free blacks settled nearby, forming the first black community in America.

THE TRENDS AND EVENTS THAT LED TO DE JURE SLAVERY

The first clear indication that the status of some blacks was changing from indentured servant to slave is the Maryland statute of 1639 that declared: "All inhabitants of this Province being Christian, slaves excepted, shall have and enjoy all such rights, liberties, privileges, and free customs within this province as any natural subject of England." The first definite de jure recognition of slavery in Virginia occurred in the case of John Punch, a black indentured servant. He, along with a Dutch servant and a Scottish servant, was retaken after escaping to Maryland in 1640. The General Court sentenced the Dutchman and the Scot to one additional year of service to their masters. The black was assigned for the rest of his life to the service of his master.

The case of John Casor also indicated a trend toward enslavement in the colony of Virginia. Casor, a black indentured servant, was brought to trial in the North Hampton County Court of Virginia by his master, Anthony Johnson. Casor claimed that he had served Johnson for fifteen years as an indentured servant and should be set free. The court decided that Casor should be assigned to Johnson as a servant for life. This case is significant historically in that Johnson, the master, was also black.

The first statutory recognition of slavery in Virginia took place in 1660. From 1660 to 1682, laws were enacted that gave legal sanction to slavery. A law of 1670, for example, provided that "all servants not being Christians" that were imported into the colony by shipping were to be slaves for life. The phrase "all servants not being Christians" referred to blacks imported directly from Africa, almost all of whom were pagans or Muslims.

One loophole in the 1670 statute was that Christian blacks from neighboring colonies, or Africans who had been converted to Christianity before reaching Virginia, had to be granted indentured status. Consequently, the General Assembly of Virginia passed a law in 1682 stating that all persons of "non-Christian nationalities" coming into Virginia, whether by land or sea, and whether or not they had been converted to Christianity after being captured in their homelands, were servants for life. A similar law had been passed earlier in Maryland to increase the importation of slaves for masters who were reluctant to give their servants religious instruction for fear of loss through emancipation. The Maryland Act of 1671 stated that conversion to Christianity did not affect the status of servants.

The white colonist had to develop a rationale for institutionalized de jure slavery. Many historians believe that discrimination against blacks preceded the economic need for their labor and that racial prejudice in America can be traced to the powerful impact that the black person's color had upon the English. "Long before the English found that some humans were black," wrote Winthrop Jordan in his book *White over Black,* "they found in the idea of blackness a way of expressing some of their more ingrained values." No other color except white conveyed so much emotional impact. The *Oxford English Dictionary* before the sixteenth century defined black as the quality of being "deeply stained with dirt; soiled, foul . . . having dark or deadly purposes, malignant; pertaining to or involving death . . . horrible, wicked." "Black was an emotionally partisan color, the handmaid and symbol of baseness and evil, a sign of danger and repulsion," wrote Jordan.

Embedded in the concept of blackness was its direct opposite, whiteness. No other color so clearly implied opposition. No other colors were used to denote polarization so frequently:

Every white will have its black
And every sweet its sowre.

Whiteness carried a special significance for the English in Elizabethan times. White was the color of perfect human beauty. By contrast, blacks were ugly, by reason of color but also because of their "horrid curles" and disfigured lips and noses. As Shakespeare wrote apologetically of his black mistress:

Tis beauty truly blent, whose red and white
Nature's own sweet and cunning hand laid on,
My mistress eyes are nothing like the sun.

Coral is far more red than her lips red.
If snow be white, why then her breasts are dun.
If hair be wires, black wires grow on her head.

I have seen roses demasked, red and white,
But no such roses see I in her cheeks.

Thus, the belief that blacks are innately inferior was brought to this country. It still survives today, in spite of scientific and historical evidence to the contrary.

LEARNING ACTIVITIES

To accomplish the objectives of this chapter, you should do the following:
A. Study the chapter Overview.
B. Read the Major Themes.
C. Read Chapter Seven in the anthology.
D. Examine carefully Section VII of the Continuity Table.
E. Answer these questions.
    1. What criteria were used by the planter class in colonial Virginia to assign indentured status to the first blacks who entered the colony?
    2. What were the factors that influenced the planter class to stop assigning indentured status to blacks entering the colonies of Virginia and Maryland after 1682?
    3. What specific cases, events, and laws can be used to trace the trend from de facto slavery to de jure slavery for blacks in colonial Virginia and Maryland?
    4. What emotional impact do the colors black and white have upon you when you use them in the context of race, race relations, or prejudiced behavior?

POSTEVALUATION

To check your learning, select the most appropriate answer to each of the following questions:
1. Africans who were taken to the colony of Virginia in the 1630s could claim indentured servant status because they
    a. came from civilized societies in Africa.
    b. had Spanish surnames.
    c. had been converted to Christianity.
    d. were devout Muslims.
2. The attempt to use white indentured servants to satisfy the labor shortage in the colonies failed because
    a. there were too many white indentured servants.
    b. they enjoyed the rights of social mobility.
    c. they were Christians.
    d. they could only be held a prescribed time.
    e. all of the above.

3. Blacks became slaves in the southern colonies during the 1650s because they
   a. were highly visible and had no rights.
   b. were considered pagans.
   c. were believed to be uncivilized.
   d. were illiterate and unable to use the laws to defend themselves.
   e. all of the above.

4. The white colonists' rationale for institutionalized de jure slavery was based upon
   a. the powerful impact that the black person's color had upon the English.
   b. the definition of black in the *Oxford English Dictionary.*
   c. the existing slave institution in England.
   d. English imperial policies.
   e. none of the above.

5. Of the following, the best evidence that prejudice and discrimination toward blacks existed in Britain is
   a. the rare intermarriage between whites and blacks.
   b. Shakespeare's sonnet about his black mistress.
   c. the definition of white in the *Oxford English Dictionary.*
   d. only (b) and (c).
   e. all of the above.

(For correct answers, see ANSWER KEY.)

ANNOTATED BIBLIOGRAPHY

Forer, Eric. *America's Black Past: A Reader in Afro-American History.* New York: Harper & Row, 1970. A well put-together anthology of selected readings of black Americans' past.

Franklin, John Hope. *From Slavery to Freedom.* New York: Knopf, 1974. The most definitive study of early black life in America. Franklin's expertise on colonial blacks makes Chapter 6 of this book important reading for every student.

Jordan, Winthrop. *White over Black.* Baltimore, Maryland: Penguin Books, 1968. Dr. Jordan's research on colonial blacks in Virginia is interesting and unique. His written accounts describe a historical past of which most Americans have been denied a knowledge. His accounts of the evolution of prejudice in America are unparalleled.

CHAPTER EIGHT

SLAVERY:
As Practiced in
the Thirteen Colonies

The inexperienced (stupid) child contends that he can tie up water with a rope. (AFRICAN PROVERB)

OVERVIEW

Slavery existed in some form in all thirteen of the American colonies. In Virginia the status of blacks was doubtful for a long period because there was no statutory recognition of slavery in that colony until 1660. The Carolina colonists never debated the question of legal slavery. The founders of that colony were interested in the use of slaves, as well as in the slave trade. In Georgia slavery was initially prohibited. The trustees of this colony did not believe that the colonists, many of whom were released from the prisons of England, could afford slaves. However, after agitation by Georgians, slavery became part of the socioeconomic life of the colony.

Slaves were commodities of commerce in the middle colonies. An unromantic patriarchal type of slavery was introduced into New Amsterdam (now New York) by the Dutch. The importance of slavery in New England was emphasized by the energy with which the Puritans entered into the business of enslaving. Even though the treatment of slaves was more humane in New England, blacks still revolted against their masters.

The Quakers were the first organized group to oppose the slave trade and ownership of slaves. Quakers exerted a moderating effect on colonial slavery practices in the colonies of North Carolina, Pennsylvania, and New Jersey.

This chapter examines early forms of slavery in the thirteen original colonies. Quaker opposition to slavery as well as slave codes and slave revolts in colonial America are also explored.

OBJECTIVES

As a result of studying this chapter, you should be able to:

1. Explain white reaction to potential slave insurrections in America by describing their response to early slave revolts in Virginia.
2. Describe slave reactions to slavery by detailing the acts of retaliation taken by slaves in colonial Maryland.
3. Analyze the role of slaves in the rivalry between Catholics and Protestants in Maryland by indicating their motives for collusion with the Catholics.
4. Describe the development of the institution of slavery in the Carolinas by contrasting slave conditions in North Carolina and South Carolina.
5. Analyze the reasons why Georgia changed from a colony that prohibited slavery to one that sanctioned it by describing Georgia colonists' reactions to the slave prohibition.
6. Discuss blacks' reactions to the slave codes in New York by delineating their response to the codes.
7. Describe the treatment of slaves by contrasting the treatment of slaves in the New England and the southern colonies.

8. Illustrate the uniqueness of slavery in New England by contrasting New England's master-slave relationship with that of the other colonies.
9. Determine the impact of the Quakers on slavery by assessing the results of their missionary activities among blacks and whites.
10. Contrast Quaker opposition to and Christian support for slavery issues in Pennsylvania by describing their ideological beliefs.

MAJOR THEMES
SLAVERY IN COLONIAL AMERICA

The black slave population of Virginia grew very slowly early in the seventeenth century. In 1625, there were twenty-three blacks in Virginia. In the latter part of the century, however, slave importation grew so rapidly that some whites became alarmed at the large slave populations within their borders.

Virginia had reasons to fear its large black population because, as early as 1663, slaves began to rebel against their masters. In 1687 a slave plot was uncovered in Northern Neck in which slaves, in an attempt to gain freedom, planned to kill all the whites in the vicinity. White masters responded to the threat by enacting slave codes, which punished blacks by whipping and branding. Before the end of the colonial period, Virginia initiated practices that attempted to keep slaves under stringent controls.

In Maryland there was little organized resistance to slavery on the part of blacks, although individual resistance was commonplace. Some black women killed their masters by feeding them ground glass. Black men burned the tobacco houses and residences of white masters. Slaves in Maryland were also factors in the religious strife in the colony. The intense rivalry between Catholics and Protestants for control of the colony was intensified by the alleged collusion of blacks with Catholics to overthrow the colonial government of Maryland.

The legality of slavery was never a question in the Carolina colonies. Proprietors offered 20 acres of land for every black male slave and 10 acres for every black female slave brought into the colony in 1663, and this offer continued for five years. Thus, the slave population grew very fast, and by the middle of the eighteenth century the large size of the black slave population was viewed with alarm.

The establishment of the colony of Georgia was based on a social experiment. George Oglethorpe persuaded the King of England to send English debtors to Georgia in order to rehabilitate them. These prisoners were also sent to act as a buffer colony between South Carolina and Spanish Florida. Indians and runaway blacks from Florida were raiding the plantations of South Carolina, causing great alarm among the prosperous South Carolinians. Since the colonists were poor, the trustees for the colony of Georgia decided that slavery would be prohibited. However, whites became discontented with the slave prohibition and engaged in lawlessness and a general strike, thus bringing about the repeal of the slave prohibition in Georgia.

The first blacks were taken to the Dutch colony of New Netherland around 1628. The blacks, who were concentrated primarily on farms in the Hudson River Valley, enjoyed fairly humane treatment. They were not restricted in their movement and were allowed to celebrate Christmas, the New Year, and what blacks called "Pinkster." When the English captured the colony of New Netherland in 1664, they renamed both the colony and its capital New York. Slavery became one of the important economic institutions of the colony. In 1701 the colonial legislature enacted a law stating that conversion to Christianity did not provide the grounds for freedom. Blacks in New York have been described by historians as having had ungovernable tempers. Consequently, the slave codes and punishments for blacks were as harsh and inhumane as those that existed in some southern colonies.

The Swedish and Dutch settlers of New Jersey were indifferent to slavery, but the English encouraged slavery in the eastern section of the colony. The black slaves of New Jersey were used in farming and mining as well as in maritime work and lumbering.

In New England a unique de facto slave system existed. The system of slavery had many characteristics of simple servitude and some features of a free society. Blacks were not subjected to harsh codes or severe treatment. Puritan respect for learning was also instrumental in making the slave system unique. Puritans attempted to convert their slaves, and the ability to read was considered necessary for true adherence to the Puritan faith.

THE IMPACT OF THE QUAKERS ON SLAVERY

The presence of Quakers had a moderating impact on the treatment of slaves by white slaveholders. Quakers were discouraged by their leaders from purchasing slaves, and in 1770 the Quaker organization began to prohibit the slave trade.

The Black Population During the Colonial Period

	1630	1640	1650	1660	1670	1680	1690	1700
North	10	427	880	1,162	1,125	1,895	3,340	5,206
South	50	170	720	1,758	3,410	5,076	13,389	22,611
Total	60	597	1,600	2,920	4,535	6,971	16,729	27,817

	1710	1720	1730	1740	1750	1760	1770	1780
North	8,303	14,091	17,323	23,958	30,222	40,033	48,460	56,796
South	36,563	54,748	73,698	126,066	206,198	285,773	411,362	518,624
Total	44,866	68,839	91,021	150,024	236,420	325,806	459,822	575,420

Quakers urged masters to convert their slaves to Christianity and to teach them to read and write the scriptures. They also sought to raise living standards among both whites and blacks.

The presence of Quakers in the western section of New Jersey, for example, improved the lot of slaves. John Woolman of Mount Holly, New Jersey, began his long, persistent opposition to slavery in 1743. By 1758 Quakers opposed not only the importation and purchase of slaves but also the possession of black people. Quakers also established schools for black children and initiated humanitarian sentiment against institutionalized slavery in New Jersey.

Blacks lived in Pennsylvania before it was purchased by William Penn. Strong objections were raised to slavery on moral and ethical grounds by Germantown Quakers in 1688. White artisans, shopkeepers, and small farmers did not feel a need for slaves and were opposed to their presence because of the disadvantages nonslaveholders suffered in competition with slave masters. These two factors produced strong opposition to the development of slavery in Pennsylvania. The mildness of slavery in Pennsylvania did not inhibit the Quakers, and later the Germans of the colony, from continuing their opposition to slavery. These groups became the leaders of the antislavery movement that would lead the fight against the further importation and possession of slaves in colonial America.

The New England Quakers, like the Puritans, advocated a policy of educating blacks. The Society of Friends provided instructors to teach young blacks to read and write. Other schools for blacks were organized in New England by interested whites. Consequently, New England blacks were the best trained and most articulate of all blacks in colonial America.

SLAVE REVOLTS IN COLONIAL AMERICA

In 1700 the northern portion of the Carolinas separated from the southern portion. In South Carolina the slave population grew so rapidly that whites became apprehensive over the large influx of blacks. Codes were established to control the slave population. In 1770 several blacks were burned alive because of their involvement in a revolt near Charles Town. In 1779 there were three slave uprisings in the colony. The most serious early revolt was the Cato conspiracy, in which slaves secured arms and ammunition and proceeded to escape to Florida and freedom.

These revolts led to a revision of the slave codes. More stringent provisions for controlling blacks were initiated. Owners were prohibited from working slaves such long hours and from performing acts of extreme cruelty. White South Carolinians realized too late that the large black population in the colony would remain a threat as long as the latter was in chains.

Insurrections recorded by slaves also took place in New York in 1712 and 1741.

The black participants in these insurrections were castrated, branded, hanged, or burned alive.

LEARNING ACTIVITIES

To accomplish the objectives of this chapter, you should do the following:
A. Study the chapter Overview.
B. Read the Major Themes.
C. Read Chapter Eight of the anthology.
D. Examine carefully Section VIII of the Continuity Table.
E. Answer these questions.
   1. Were black slaves justified in using any and all means necessary to secure their freedom?
   2. Why did most Protestant churches, as Christian institutions, fail to attack slavery?
   3. How could a Protestant minister be a Christian and a slaveholder?
   4. What factors might be used to explain the different treatment slaves received in the southern, middle, and New England colonies?

POSTEVALUATION

To check your learning, select the most appropriate answer to each of the following questions:
1. Virginian slave owners increasingly feared massive slave revolts because of
   a. the existence of a large free black population.
   b. the large slave black population.
   c. acts of destruction by blacks.
   d. white support for black emancipation.
   e. all of the above.
2. Slaves were accused of attempting to overthrow the government in Maryland because of their collusion with
   a. Catholics.
   b. Protestants.
   c. Indians.
   d. free blacks.
   e. abolitionists.
3. The slave codes in New York, in comparison with those of some southern colonies, were
   a. more severe.
   b. less severe.
   c. equally as severe.
   d. not a factor, because slave codes did not really exist in New York.

4. Slavery did not become institutionalized in New Jersey and Pennsylvania because
   a. the Swedish and Dutch settlers were indifferent to slavery.
   b. Quakers presented opposition to slavery.
   c. there was widespread objection to slavery on moral grounds.
   d. competition existed between slave masters and white laborers.
   e. all of the above.
5. Which of the following is *not* a reason for the mildness of slavery in New England in contrast to other regions?
   a. Blacks and whites had higher levels of education.
   b. Blacks and whites worked side by side.
   c. The urban nature of the New England terrain did not necessitate the use of slaves.
   d. The size of the slave population was large.

(For correct answers, see ANSWER KEY.)

ANNOTATED BIBLIOGRAPHY

Current, Richard, T. Henry Williams, and Frank Freidel. *American History.* New York: Knopf, 1975. This book provides a traditional look at colonial America. It is useful in supplying information on the general feelings of the colonists and trends of the colonial period.

Franklin, John Hope. *From Slavery to Freedom.* New York: Knopf, 1974. This book is the revised edition of Franklin's monumental work. The author's description of black life in the thirteen colonies is matchless.

CHAPTER NINE

REVOLUTIONARY PHILOSOPHY:
Its Impact on Slavery

When deeds speak, words are nothing.
(AFRICAN PROVERB)

OVERVIEW

The doctrine of natural law, the notion that human rights transcend the powers of government, became the philosophy of American revolutionaries. This philosophy of freedom was incompatible, however, with slavery and other forms of discrimination. Some Americans realized that they could not, in good conscience, condemn England for curtailing their liberties if they were themselves guilty of oppressing blacks in America.

James Otis was one of the first colonists to affirm the American blacks' natural right to freedom, in *The Rights of the British Colonies Asserted and Proved*. Blacks began to link the revolutionary fervor of the American colonists to their own status by petitioning the colonial legislatures for their freedom.

Crispus Attucks, a runaway slave, was one of the first revolutionists to die for his country (on March 5, 1770, in Boston). More than 5,000 black men eventually served in the colonial army. Initially, they were prohibited from enlisting by General George Washington. Later, when manpower needs were acute, discriminatory practices were dropped and black soldiers were allowed to join the army. Black soldiers played an important role in bringing victory and independence to the United States of America.

This chapter discusses colonial inconsistencies of thought and action in relation to black rights. It also examines the Declaration of Independence, black participation in the Revolutionary War, and black inventive and literary contributions to America in that era.

OBJECTIVES

As a result of studying this chapter, you should be able to:

1. Determine the importance of the doctrine of natural law to the philosophy of the American Revolution by stating its three basic principles.
2. Analyze the philosophical basis of the Declaration of Independence by describing Jefferson's rationale for separation from England.
3. Evaluate Jefferson's philosophy of freedom and slavery by reading the sections of the Declaration of Independence he was forced to delete.
4. State the inconsistency between the revolutionary philosophy and justifications for slavery by contrasting the principles upon which each is based.
5. Explain the basis for the view that Crispus Attucks was a revolutionary martyr by describing his role in the Boston Massacre.
6. Describe the role of black Minutemen by listing the battlefield accomplishments of Peter Salem and Salem Poor.
7. Discuss the reasons for General Washington's ban on black enlistments and reenlistments of blacks by delineating the sentiments of slaveholders toward black participation in the Revolutionary War.

8. Analyze General Washington's decision to lift the ban on black enlistment into the army by describing the impact on the Continental Congress of Lord Dunmore's decree.
9. Assess the scientific impact of colonial blacks such as Benjamin Banneker by stating his contributions.

MAJOR THEMES
THE ROOTS OF THE AMERICAN REVOLUTION

The American Revolution originated as a response to the economic policies of the British Parliament. Parliament initiated policies designed to increase the political and economic dependence of the American colonists. The British Prime Minister's proposals would force the colonists to assume a larger portion of the tax burden caused by the French and Indian War, which ended in 1763. The colonists argued that Parliament did not directly represent their interest and, therefore, had no power to tax them.

The period from 1765 through 1775 was characterized by growing tensions and hostilities between England and the American colonies. British imperialistic policies threatened the political and economic freedom of the colonies. The American leaders sought to justify their opposition to the British by stressing the revolutionary literature written by Jean Jacques Rousseau and John Locke.

THE IMPACT OF THE WRITINGS OF JOHN LOCKE

Locke's concept of natural law stressed the rights of life, liberty, and the pursuit of happiness; the primacy of the individual; and the social equality of all human beings. These revolutionary ideas were instrumental in forcing some leaders to recognize the marked inconsistency between the colonists' protest as an oppressed people and their position as slaveholders. The concept of natural law received its most significant expression in 1776 in the Declaration of Independence, which was primarily the work of Thomas Jefferson.

JEFFERSON'S ATTACK ON SLAVERY

In the original draft of the Declaration of Independence Jefferson identified the abuses the colonists had suffered at the hands of the British. He also accused King George III of England of encouraging the slave trade and suppressing colonial legislative attempts to prohibit it. Jefferson's specific charges against King George III were as follows:

He has waged cruel war against human nature itself, violating its most sacred rights of life and liberty in the person of a distant people who never offended him, captivating and carrying them into slavery in another hemisphere, or to incur miserable death in their transportation thither. This piratical warfare, the opprobrium of infidel powers, is the warfare of the Christian King of Great Britain. Determined to keep open a market where MEN should be bought and sold, he has prostituted his negative for suppressing every legislative attempt to prohibit or to restrain this execrable commerce; and that this assemblage of horrors might want no fact of distinguished due, he is now exciting these very people to rise in arms among us, and to purchase that liberty of which he deprived them, by murdering the people upon whom he also obtruded them; thus paying off former crimes committed against the liberties of one people, with crimes which he urges them to commit against the lives of another.

The attack on the slave trade in the original draft of the Declaration was unacceptable to the southern delegation to the Continental Congress and was stricken. Slaveholders realized that, if Jefferson's attack on slavery remained in the Declaration of Independence, there would be no legal or moral justification for retaining slavery if the Revolution succeeded.

BLACK CONTRIBUTIONS DURING THE REVOLUTIONARY ERA

Prior to the colonists' Declaration of Independence, Crispus Attucks was killed in the Boston Massacre of March 1770. Attucks was a black runaway slave from Framingham, Massachusetts, who had become a sailor in the colonial maritime industry. Attucks was one of the leaders of a crowd of colonial demonstrators who were protesting the presence of British occupation soldiers in Boston. Words were exchanged, blows were struck, and British soldiers fired into the crowd, killing Attucks, Samuel Grey, Samuel Maverick, and James Caldwell.

Bostonians were stirred by the sacrifice of this black rebel who had joined them in their fight for freedom, even though he was not himself free. Some, like Abigail Adams, protested the contradiction inherent in the spectacle of slave masters seeking freedom from England and at the same time holding blacks in bondage.

The dilemma of white colonists in the wake of Attucks' death was intensified by the participation of quasi-free and enslaved blacks in the Revolutionary War. Black Minutemen, such as Prince Esterbrooks at the Battle of Lexington and Peter Salem at Concord and Bunker (Breeds) Hill, typify the service of blacks in the War of Independence.

Peter Salem was born a slave. Even though blacks were excluded from the colonial militia by law, some were admitted because of manpower shortages.

Patriot Soldiers

Most Americans are not aware of the black soldiers who fought at the Battle of Bunker (Breeds) Hill on June 17, 1775. They were Peter Salem, Salem Poor, Titus Coburn, Cato Howe, Alexander Ames, Seymour Burr, Pomp Fiske, and Prince Hall.

Hence, blacks like Peter Salem enlisted in Minuteman companies. In the militia's of the New England colonies freedom was given to most blacks if they were successful in enlisting. Salem Poor, another black man, was decorated for bravery at Bunker Hill. Poor's commanding officer signed a petition and sent it to the Massachusetts legislature on December 5, 1775, stating:

> The subscribers beg to report to your Honorable House that, under our own observation, we declare that a negro man called Salem Poor, of Col. Frye's regiment, Capt. Ames company, in the late battle at Charleston (Bunker Hill), behaved like an experienced officer, as well as an excellent soldier. . . . In the person of this said negro centres a brave and gallant soldier. The reward due to so great and distinguished a character, we submit to the Congress.

Southern delegates to the Continental Congress opposed the participation by blacks in the war. General Washington, upon taking command of the Continental Army, issued instructions to recruiting officers on July 10, 1775, forbidding the enlistment of any more blacks. Those blacks who enlisted prior to the ban could continue to serve but would not be allowed to reenlist. The British, however, used blacks in their war effort. On November 7, 1775, John Murray, Lord of Dunmore, the royal governor, proclaimed freedom for all blacks who joined the king's army.

General Washington was alarmed when slaves in Virginia began to support the British forces. On December 30, 1775, Washington was forced to drop the ban against the use of black soldiers when manpower needs became more demanding than personal prejudices. Consequently, more than 5,000 blacks served in the Continental Army in all the state regiments except those of Georgia and South Carolina, which refused to allow blacks to join the militia. With the exception of three or four all-black fighting regiments, blacks served in both the army and the navy in integrated units.

BLACK LITERARY AND SCIENTIFIC FIGURES DURING THE REVOLUTIONARY WAR ERA

During the Revolutionary War era blacks had increasing opportunities to demonstrate their abilities, to secure an education and training, and to make important contributions to America. Many of these contributions were made by anonymous black craftsmen and artists. But some black poets, such as Lucy Terry and Jupiter Hammond, became well known. Of all the early black achievers, however, none was more prominent than Phillis Wheatley or Benjamin Banneker.

Phillis Wheatley was hailed as proof of what blacks could accomplish if given the chance. She composed poems in the style of Alexander Pope in a book titled *Poems on Various Subjects, Religious and Moral,* published in 1773. Typical of her style is one of the more famous poems from that collection, "On Being Brought from Africa to America":

Twas mercy brought me from my pagan land
Taught my benighted soul to understand
That there's a God, that there's a Savior too;
Once I redemption neither sought nor knew,
Some view our sable race with scornful eye,
Their color is a diabolic die.
Remember, Christians, Negroes, Black as Cain,
May be refined, and join th' angelic train.

Although a slave, Phillis Wheatley was never mistreated and was considered a member of the share-owning Wheatley family. Despite the great kindness of her master, Phillis wanted freedom, as she described it in this poem:

Should you, my Lord, while you peruse my song,
Wonder from whence my love of freedom sprung,
Whence flow these wishes for the common good,
By feeling hearts alone best understood,
I, young in life, by seeming cruel fate
Was snatch'd from Afri's fancy'd happy seat.
What pangs excruciating must molest,
What sorrows labour in my parents' breast?
Steel'd was the soul and by no misery mov'd
That from a father seiz'd his babe belov'd:
Such, such my case. And can I then but pray
Others may never feel tryannic sway?

Phillis Wheatley also wrote a poem entitled "His Excellency General Washington," in which she praised Washington's leadership.

Benjamin Banneker was born free in the slave colony of Maryland and attended an integrated Quaker school. His mathematical abilities were recognized very early by the leading mathematicians of the colonies. In 1761 Banneker made a clock out of wooden parts. He also mastered astronomy and wrote an annual almanac. Early in 1791 Banneker was appointed by President George Washington to serve with French Major Pierre-Charles L'Enfant and Andrew Ellicott, III, to plan the new federal capital in the District of Columbia. When L'Enfant left the job undone, the task fell to Banneker and Ellicott to complete laying out Washington, D.C.

RESULTS OF BLACK CONTRIBUTIONS

The contributions and sacrifices of blacks led to their emancipation in the northern states after the Revolution. The early antislavery movement reached a peak with the passage of the Northwest Ordinance of 1787, which prohibited slavery

The Three-fifths Compromise: Article I, Section 2
Representatives and direct Taxes shall be apportioned among the several States which may be included within this Union, according to their respective Numbers, which shall be determined by adding to the whole number of free Persons, including those bound to Service for a Term of Years, and excluding Indians not taxed, three fifths of all other Persons.

The Northwest Ordinance of July 13, 1787
Article G. There shall be neither slavery nor involuntary servitude in the said territory, otherwise than in the punishment of crimes whereof the party shall have been duly convicted: Provided, always, that any person escaping into same, from labor or service is lawfully claimed in any one of the original States, such fugitive may be lawfully reclaimed and conveyed to the person claiming his or her labor or service as aforesaid.

The Constitution Legalizes the Slave Trade: Article I, Section 9
The Migration or Importation of such persons as any of the States now existing shall think proper to admit, shall not be prohibited by the Congress prior to the Year one thousand eight hundred and eight, but a tax or duty may be imposed on such Importation, not exceeding ten dollars for each Person.

north of the Ohio River. The Constititution of 1787, however, recognized slavery by the Three-fifths Compromise. That document also placed restrictions on congressional interference with the African slave trade for two decades and provided for the return of fugitive slaves. The Constitution did not contain such words as slaves or African, black or Negro, but everyone knew to whom Article I, Sections 2 and 9, and Article IV, Section 2 of the Constitution referred.

Later, in *Notes on Virginia*, Thomas Jefferson would reflect upon institutionalized slavery in America by writing:

Indeed, I tremble for my country when I reflect God is just. That his justice cannot sleep forever, that considering numbers, nature and natural means only, a revolution of the wheel of fortune, an exchange of station is among possible events. Nothing is more certainly written in the book of fate than these people are to be free, only the means are at question. White men must liberate Negroes in Justice or Negroes would liberate themselves in blood.

LEARNING ACTIVITIES

To accomplish the objectives of this chapter, you should do the following:

A. Study the chapter Overview.
B. Study the Major Themes.
C. Read Chapter Nine of the anthology.
D. Examine carefully Section IX of the Continuity Table.
E. Answer these questions.
    1. What are the basic principles of human rights which natural laws embody?
    2. Why were enslaved and quasi-free blacks, such as Crispus Attucks and Salem Poor, willing to fight and die for American independence?
    3. Why did southern colonists force Thomas Jefferson to delete his attack on slavery from the original draft of the Declaration of Independence?
    4. What were scme of the literary and scientific contributions of colonial blacks during the period from 1776 through 1800?
    5. Why was the word "slave" not used in sections of the Constitution that legalized the institution of slavery?

POSTEVALUATION

To check your learning, select the most appropriate answer to each of the following questions:
1. Which of the following was *not* included in John Locke's concept of natural law upon which American claims to independence were based?
    a. The right of life.
    b. The pursuit of happiness.
    c. The primacy of the individual.
    d. The social equality of all men.
    e. The collective responsibility of government.
2. According to Thomas Jefferson, who was at fault for the perpetuation of slavery?
    a. The American colonists, who refused to engage in hard work.
    b. King George III of England, who suppressed colonial attempts to prohibit slavery.
    c. Northern abolitionists, who offended southern slaveholders by challenging their Christianity.
    d. General George Washington, who also owned slaves himself.
3. Why were New Englanders the first colonists to realize that desiring freedom for themselves was inconsistent with holding blacks in bondage?
    a. The educational level of slaves and whites was higher in New England than in the other colonies.
    b. Slavery was only a de facto institution in New England; there was no legal basis for it.
    c. City environment provided more positive contacts between black slaves and whites in New England.

    d. Black slaves were willing to fight for the country's freedom even though they themselves were not free.

    e. All of the above.

4. All of the following were central themes of Phillis Wheatley's poem on freedom *except:*

    a. her rejection of being enslaved, even by kindly masters.

    b. her happiness as a slave with the Wheatleys.

    c. her loss of freedom as a cruel fate.

    d. the sorrow her parents felt when she was taken from them.

    e. her former happiness in being free in Africa.

5. The Constitution of 1789 legitimatized slavery by

    a. the Three-fifths Compromise.

    b. restricting congressional interference in the slave trade.

    c. providing for returning fugitive slaves.

    d. extending slave importations until 1808.

    e. all of the above.

(For correct answers, see ANSWER KEY.)

ANNOTATED BIBLIOGRAPHY

Fishels, Leslie, and Benjamin Quarles. *The Negro American, A Documentary History.* New York: William Morrow , 1967. This book provides the reader with primary historical sources. Each historical source begins with a brief summary that guides the reader through enjoyable readings.

Franklin, John Hope. *From Slavery to Freedom.* New York: Knopf, 1974. Dr. Franklin's description of the Revolutionary era is well written and very readable. The description of Thomas Jefferson's original draft of the Declaration is must reading for every student.

Kaplan, Sidney. *The Black Presence in the Era of the American Revolution 1770–1800.* New York: Graphic Society, 1973. An excellent scholarly work on the role of blacks in the revolutionary period.

Smith, Page. *A New Age Now Begins: A People's History of the American Revolution.* New York: McGraw-Hill, 1976. This is a well-documented account of the American Revolution. The author does an exceptional job of including blacks' participation in his overall historical accounts.

CHAPTER TEN

PLANTATION LIFE:
Emergence of
a Culture

Lack of companionship is worse than poverty.
(AFRICAN PROVERB)

OVERVIEW

Slave labor in America was primarily agricultural; consequently, most slaves worked and lived on farms and plantations. The greatest number were on cotton plantations, and the remainder were involved primarily in the cultivation of tobacco, rice, and sugar cane. Most plantations were small and had only a few slaves. When this was the case, owners and slaves worked the fields together, side by side. Some plantations were large enough to require elaborate organization, including hired overseers to supervise and monitor slave labor.

On the larger plantations a hierarchy of prestige and status developed among the slaves. There were house slaves and field slaves. The house slaves, as the name indicates, took care of the master's house—its surroundings as well as its inhabitants. Their job included safeguarding the health and welfare of the master's family. Intimate bonds often developed between house slaves and masters. As a result, house slaves enjoyed better clothing, better food, and better treatment than their counterparts who worked in the fields.

Field hands were low in the hierarchy. Their work was more oppressive and more physically demanding. They worked long, hard hours under close supervision and were instructed as to when to start work, when to eat, and when to stop work. Men, women, and children worked the fields and were subject to merciless driving by the overseer and to severe punishment for unsatisfactory performance.

In their attempts to survive and to endure the physical and psychological traumas that life on the plantation presented, slaves developed a distinct plantation culture. Cultural patterns that emerged on the plantation formed the core of black American culture and contributed to the development of American culture in general.

This chapter examines the components of the plantation culture that emerged. It focuses on the institutions, the patterns, and the rituals that the slaves developed or engaged in to make their lives on the plantation tolerable.

OBJECTIVES

As a result of studying this chapter, you should be able to:
1. Describe the hierarchy that existed among plantation slaves by contrasting the status of house slaves with that of field slaves.
2. Discuss the emergence of plantation culture by describing how slaves coped with the physical and psychological cruelties they encountered.
3. Indicate the difficulty plantation slaves had in surviving by noting the conditions under which they lived from day to day.
4. Discuss the many functions of religion on the plantations by specifying the needs that it met for the slaves and their masters.
5. Refute the argument that slave speech represented slave inability to learn

proper English by pointing to the basis of slave speech.

6. Show the tool-like nature of slave spirituals by describing their various uses.
7. Describe the African influence upon the plantation culture by isolating specific African influences in that culture.

MAJOR THEMES

DAILY LIFE

Slaves were faced with both physical and psychological cruelties on the plantation. Field hand overseers were responsible for much of the physical brutality. The overseer's whip was forever present and lashed out indiscriminately. Slaves were beaten for not working, for not working hard or fast enough, for stealing, for running away, or for doing whatever a master or overseer felt was inappropriate.

Although the beatings were cruel, perhaps the harshest aspects of slavery were the psychological cruelties. The fact that a person was not free meant that he or she could have no control over his or her fate. It meant that family units could be broken up, children sold away from parents, or husbands sold away from wives at the whims of slave masters. It meant a precarious existence.

Living conditions on plantations varied. Some slaves were well fed, well clothed, and well cared for when ill, but most were not. Homes were one-room log cabins, poorly furnished and poorly ventilated. Minimal health standards were maintained. The slaves' diet consisted primarily of pork, chicken, corn meal, vegetables, and occasionally beef. Few slaves starved, but many were malnourished. Clothing was simple but most often adequate.

Slave quarters were separate from the master's dwelling. The slaves formed a community, which fostered love and respect among its members. It was a cohesive base of support for all its members and provided orientation for its new members. A large part of black American culture had its origin in the slave community.

RELIGION

Most slaves embraced evangelical Protestantism and called themselves either Baptists or Methodists. The expression of religious fervor was emotionally intense on the plantation. The mourners' bench, the shouting, the hand clapping, the foot stomping, the holy dancing, and the fervent "amens" gave black religion a rich atmosphere of excitement. The religious meeting provided not only spiritual inspiration but also greatly needed social outlets. Relaxation, good food, gossip, and general socializing were provided at religious gatherings.

The church offered one of the few opportunities for black leadership. Highly respected black preachers were the focal point of solidarity. They used their sermons as a spiritual, as well as an informational, medium. Through this medium, they stressed freedom, human dignity, and self-respect. Few of the early black preachers were educated; many were completely illiterate and were referred to as "jack leg" preachers.

Black preachers sometimes held secondary roles to the "conjure men," who could cast spells, predict the future, heal the sick, and make love potions. They helped to preserve an African tradition, "root work."

Whites tried to maintain surveillance over black religious gatherings, fearing that religious autonomy would invite rebellion. They bombarded the slaves with Christian teachings that stressed submission. "Blessed are the obedient" was a favorite expression of slave masters. Christianity did not instill submission in all slaves but instead it served as a source of resistance in many instances.

SPEECH PATTERNS

Plantation slaves, for the most part, did not speak standard English. Instead, they spoke what has come to be called "black English" or "black dialect." Early historians suggested that slaves were inferior to Europeans and, thus, could not learn to speak proper English. Research indicates, however, that the language patterns used by slaves resulted from their placing new vocabulary into their own African language patterns. Thus, slave dialect, often berated for absence of gender, subject, or verb and for mispronunciations of words and letters, was really an expression of English or French words in an African grammatical form. These same patterns are evident in black dialect today.

MUSIC, DANCE, AND STORIES

On the plantation, as in Africa, there was a closeness in the relationship between blacks and their music. Music was an integral part of the slaves' daily life, during their work, during whatever play or free time they had, during their sorrow, joy, and anger. Music was a means by which slaves could rise above their physical existence and maintain dignity in the face of widespread rebuke.

The spiritual, unique to America, was developed by the slaves on southern plantations. The spirituals, or "sorrow songs" as W. E. B. Du Bois called them, reflected every aspect of the slaves' existence: their dreams, concerns, love, emotions, relationship with whites. Spirituals were used as codes to help slaves escape or to send messages from one plantation to another without slave owners' knowledge, in much the same fashion as drums were used for communication in Africa.

The slaves' dancing, like their singing, was active and spirited. Slave boys and girls learned to sing and dance at very early ages. These activities, however, cannot be attributed to inherited or God-given talents. The cultural environment sparked the desire and the need to learn to sing and dance. Such dances as the jig, double shuffle, cakewalk, turkey trot, and the Charleston demonstrated energy in motion. Slave dances reflected blacks' African heritage, just as did their other musical expressions.

Storytelling was a favorite and enjoyable pastime among the slaves on the plantation. The tales told were permeated with talking animals, another example of African origins in plantation culture. The Uncle Remus tales, later popularized by Joel Chandler Harris, were the most loved accounts.

These tales expressed a variety of attitudes and feelings. What could not be said to the master directly was often stated indirectly in stories. The hare and the tortoise were important symbols in black folklore. Although the hare was weak, his agility assured protection. The tortoise was slow but enduring, which brought success. To survive the weaker animals used their wit, deceit, and cunning—characteristics needed by slaves in their own struggles for survival.

LEARNING ACTIVITIES

To accomplish the objectives for this chapter, you should do the following:
A. Study the chapter Overview.
B. Read the Major Themes.
C. Read Chapter Ten in the anthology.
D. Examine carefully Section X in the Continuity Table.
E. Answer these questions.
   1. Would you have preferred to be a house slave or a field slave? Why?
   2. What was the nature of the relationships that existed between house and field slaves?
   3. What physical and psychological cruelties did plantation slaves endure?
   4. What defense mechanisms did they devise to cope with these cruelties?
   5. How did slave living conditions compare with those of their masters?
   6. What purposes did monitoring slave church meetings serve for slave masters?
   7. What functions did religious gatherings serve for the slaves?
   8. What was the role of the black preacher in the slave community?
   9. How did black dialect or slave speech develop?
   10. Compare the use of spirituals to the use of African talking drums.
   11. What are some African influences evident in plantation culture?
   12. Was the development of a plantation culture inevitable? Why or why not?

POSTEVALUATION

To check your learning, select the most appropriate answer to each of the following questions:
1. Black preachers were important to the slave community because
   a. they assumed leadership for civil rights.

b. they were the focal point of solidarity.

c. they provided spiritual inspiration.

d. they were in a position to stay abreast of "current events" affecting the slaves' lives.

e. all of the above.

2. Whites attended black religious gatherings in order to

a. convince slaves that they shared a common religious fervor.

b. provide slaves with Christian teachings.

c. inhibit slave rebellion.

d. all of the above.

3. Spirituals served a dual purpose in the slave community. They were used for

a. plantation work songs as well as for lullabies.

b. expressing emotions as well as for passing messages to help slaves escape.

c. signaling the master as well as for plantation work songs.

d. none of the above.

4. That slave boys and girls learned to dance and sing at a very early age can be attributed to

a. an inherited trait among blacks.

b. a God-given talent among slaves.

c. a desire and need to do so.

d. extra economic benefits.

e. none of the above.

5. Which of the following reflected the influence of African culture?

a. The daily meals.

b. The slave speech patterns.

c. The slave clothing.

d. The slave dwellings.

e. All of the above.

(For correct answers, see ANSWER KEY.)

ANNOTATED BIBLIOGRAPHY

Bennett, Lerone. *Before the Mayflower: A History of the Negro in America 1619–1966.* Chicago: Johnson Publishing, 1966. This is a good, popularized black history. Its narrative is colorful, readable, and accurate. Descriptions of slave life are vivid.

Berlin, Ira. *Slaves Without Masters: The Free Negro in the Antebellum South.* New York: Vintage Books, 1974. An in-depth analysis of free blacks in the South. The author makes clear that free blacks lived under oppressive conditions.

Blassingame, John W. *The Slave Community: Plantation.* New York: Oxford University Press, 1972. One of the best treatments of the institution of slavery. The value of the work lies in its extensive use of black accounts of the nature of slavery. Blassingame offers an alternative to the "Sambo" personality thesis.

Butcher, Margaret Just. *The Negro in American Culture.* New York: New American

Library, 1971. A detailed study of the conditions that led to blacks' contributions to the majority culture.

Elkins, Stanley M. *Slavery: A Problem in American Institutional and Intellectual Life.* Chicago: The University of Chicago Press, 1958. A superior work that discusses the effects of the plantation on the slave's personality. Elkins' book has come under attack because of his "Sambo" thesis.

Herskovits, Melville. *The Myth of the Negro Past.* Boston: Beacon Press, 1969. A study of the many African influences and their significance in black American culture and in American culture in general.

CHAPTER ELEVEN

NONSLAVE STATUS: Freedom vs. Quasi-Freedom

He who sleeps in the jungle is aware of the leopard.
(AFRICAN PROVERB)

OVERVIEW

Not all blacks who came to the New World came in chains. The blacks who arrived first came under conditions similar to the whites: as indentured servants. Later in history, blacks in some colonies fell into a well-established socioeconomic position that carried few implications of racial inferiority. They acquired land, voted, testified in court, and interacted with whites on an equal basis. This period is often considered to be the only period in the history of America when blacks were indeed free. The advent of slavery, however, denied blacks that degree of freedom for years.

By 1790 there were about 59,000 blacks in the United States who were free. Some 40 percent lived in the South, 46 percent in the North, and the others in the developing West. The passage from slavery to freedom happened in various ways. Some were set free by their masters or willed free upon their master's death, some bought their freedom from their masters, some were born of free mothers, and others escaped from slavery to freedom. In addition, some northern states prohibited slavery, while others worked toward gradual emancipation. The equalitarian philosophy of the Revolution furthered the cause of freedom for the blacks.

The presence of an increasing number of free blacks became a source of great anxiety to slaveholders, because it undermined the very basis on which slavery was built. In response to this inconsistency, a campaign against free blacks was carried on. The hope was to "keep them in their place." The status of the nonslave blacks was, therefore, not freedom but quasi-freedom.

This chapter describes the nature of that campaign and the resistance to it. It also identifies the blacks who managed to live, work, and contribute to American society despite the traumas of quasi-freedom.

OBJECTIVES

As a result of studying this chapter, you should be able to:
1. Explain how blacks became free in a period of black slavery and servitude by listing the various ways that freedom was achieved.
2. Assess the impact of the presence of free blacks on a slave society by discussing the responses to free blacks in the North and in the South.
3. Discuss the precarious existence of free blacks by describing how their lives were dependent upon the favor of whites.
4. Establish that "free blacks" was a misnomer, by describing state and community controls or other restraints on nonslave blacks.
5. Identify inconsistencies in the judicial system by contrasting the treatment and protection given to white citizens with those given to black citizens.
6. Recognize the difficulty that free blacks had in establishing economic stabil-

ity by describing the physical and psychological restraints they encountered.

7. Describe how free blacks earned a living by listing occupations and professions in which they achieved success.

8. Discuss the foundations from which free black families evolved by describing the lines of social relations upon which marriages were built.

9. Analyze the impact of increased educational opportunities on the lives of free blacks by identifying specific results of those educational opportunities.

10. Discuss the role of free blacks in the growth of America by identifying black contributors and their respective contributions in Western expansion and in America's wars.

MAJOR THEMES
QUASI-FREEDOM

No matter where free blacks lived, the nature of their lives depended upon the favor of whites. Free blacks found that whites could fraudulently claim them as slaves. Free blacks were often kidnapped, lowered in status, reenslaved, or sentenced by court to slavery or servitude. In southern states free blacks were required to have passes and certificates of freedom. Some states required registration; still others required free blacks to have white guardians.

State control over the free blacks' movement increased as the years went by. Free blacks' legal status gradually deteriorated, until there ceased to be much of a distinction between being free and being a slave. Laws similar to the slave codes grew in their controlling powers to restrict the movement of free blacks. Most northern and southern states had immigration laws that either restricted or

---

Certificate of Freedom

In most southern states, free blacks were required to carry a certificate of freedom on their person at all times. The contents of the freedom certificate follow. Some places provided printed forms; in others the certificates were handwritten by court clerks.

In _____ County Clerk's Office, __day/month__ 18 year (name of black), a free (man/woman) of color, who has been heretofore registered in the said office, this day delivered up to me (his/her) former certificate of registration and applied for a renewal of the same, which is granted (him/her), and (he/she) is now of the following description, to wit: age _____ years, color _____, stature _____ feet. No. 4819

In testimony whereof I have hereunto set my hand and affixed the Seal of the said County Court this _____ day of _____ A. D. one thousand, eight hundred and _____. Signed _____

forbade possession of firearms without a license. Some forbade the right of assembly without the presence of whites. By implication, then, free blacks were denied the right to hold church services unless whites were present. There were laws minimizing contact between free blacks and slaves, which in some instances led to stresses and strains in family relations.

By the beginning of the nineteenth century free blacks had lost their civil rights. In most states they lost the right to vote, as well as any kind of political influence. Yet they were required to assume the responsibilities of citizenship. They paid school taxes, even though their children could not attend school. They rarely received the protection of the justice system due any citizen. Consequently, they were attacked by mobs, their homes and churches were destroyed, and they were often run out of town. Legislative attempts were made to lighten the burden of free blacks by providing them with the opportunity to choose their masters and reenslave themselves.

ECONOMIC LIFE AMONG FREE BLACKS

There were any number of physical and psychological restraints that made it difficult for free blacks to earn a living. The psychological aspect stemmed from the difficulty in adjusting to self-providing freedom after years and years of dependent slavery. Entering the competitive labor market also presented some problems: there was heavy white opposition to black artisans; blacks were barred from certain occupations and professions; the majority of free blacks were not skilled workers and had to settle for available common labor jobs.

James Derham, born a slave in Philadelphia, is recognized as the first black doctor in America. He served as an assistant to his physician master and learned medicine from him. Derham eventually bought his freedom and established a practice. He served both blacks and whites. By 1788, he was one of the top physicians in New Orleans. Another well-known physician, Dr. Benjamin Rush, said of Derham, "I have conversed with him upon most of the acute and epidemic diseases of the country where he lives. I expected to have suggested some new medicines to him, but he suggested many more to me."

Madame C. J. Walker was founder of the world's oldest black cosmetics company. She was a financial genius whose business methods were widely copied, and she became the first black woman millionaire. She started her business with two dollars and an original formula for "refining the scalp and straightening hair."

Despite these odds, free blacks, skilled and unskilled, managed to survive and some did surprisingly well in a variety of fields. Blacks worked as confectioners, grocers, paperhangers, druggists, tailors, machinists. They worked in the building and shipping trades. They were carpenters, barbers, brickmasons, jewelers, architects, engravers, and lithographers. In some places blacks were permitted to go to school and thus entered the fields of the ministry, education, dentistry, and law. Several excelled in their occupations and even managed to accumulate considerable wealth.

FAMILY LIFE AMONG FREE BLACKS

Free blacks were not always bound by the same social controls as the rest of the free society. Therefore, their families evolved in what were seen as unconventional patterns of obtaining a license and having a civil or religious ceremony. Many families, however, resulted from marriages of free blacks and slaves. Such a marriage, which took place with the consent of the slavemaster, was deemed a casual union and no license was involved. Other free black families resulted from unions of free blacks with whites or Indians. These unions were considered informal and often illegal.

EDUCATION AND FREE BLACKS

Free blacks in the North benefited from widening educational opportunities in the nineteenth century. In some places black children attended white public schools. In other places separate schools were provided. Free blacks in the South faced more difficulties. Educating youth in the South was mostly a private family matter. There was little interest in public education and practically no interest in the education of blacks. In fact, southern states passed laws which made it illegal to teach free blacks. Nevertheless, many free blacks received instruction, but very little of it in schools. There were also free blacks who went to the North, or to Canada, or abroad for an education. Some blacks, especially in the North, managed to gain entrance to and be graduated from colleges and universities.

These educational opportunities resulted in a free black population that was better informed, more articulate, and more vocal than before. Blacks expressed their views, feelings, and aspirations in several ways. They formed associations, held conventions, published newspapers, and wrote books, including autobiographies, histories, and novels. Many of the black writings, particularly in the newspapers, were concerned with the antislavery movement.

FREE BLACKS AND WESTERN EXPANSION

From the onset of American expansion to the West, free blacks were actively involved in the process just as were black slaves. In the profitable western fur

Paul Cuffe, a free black, early in life had an interest in commerce and secured employment on a whaling vessel in 1775 at age sixteen. On his second voyage he was captured and detained by the British. During the Revolution he refused to pay taxes in Massachusetts because he was denied the franchise. Soon after, Massachusetts passed legislation allowing to those free blacks liable to taxation all the privileges that other citizens had. So, in 1780, Cuffe began shipbuilding and engaged in commerce. By 1806 he had several ships and vessels and considerable property. He was deeply concerned with the welfare of blacks and wanted to improve their lot. In 1811 he investigated the possibilities of returning free blacks to Africa. In 1815 he took thirty-eight blacks to Africa at an expense of three to four thousand dollars to himself. He learned that the expense of returning blacks to Africa was too great to be a viable solution to improving their lot.

trade, blacks often served as a liaison between whites and Indians. They were invaluable in the trade for their roles as guides, hunters, and interpreters. Several blacks became outstanding trappers and traders. There were others involved in Western expansion; among them were cowboys, explorers, and missionaries. And hundreds of other blacks, most of them obscure, contributed to the development of the American West.

FREE BLACKS AND AMERICAN WARS

Blacks, both slave and free, have participated in American wars. After the disastrous winter of Valley Forge, blacks were welcomed into the colonial army. Black soldiers from every one of the thirteen colonies fought in the Revolutionary War, many of them in integrated units. Blacks took part in the land and water battles of the War of 1812. Blacks served in the Confederacy, in the Union Army, and in the Union Navy.

Two battalions of black soldiers were with Andrew Jackson when he defeated the British at the Battle of New Orleans. He issued his famous proclamation of December 18, 1814: "TO THE MEN OF COLOR—Soldiers! From the shores of Mobile I collected you to arms; I invited you to share in the perils and to divide the glory of your white countrymen. I expected much from you, for I was not uninformed of those qualities which must render you so formidable to an invading foe. I knew that you could endure hunger and thirst and all the hardships of war. I knew that you loved the land of your nativity, and that like ourselves, you have to defend all that is most dear to you. But you surpass my hopes. I have found in you, united to these qualities, that noble enthusiasm which impels to great deeds."

LEARNING ACTIVITIES

To accomplish the objectives of this chapter, you should do the following:

A. Study the chapter Overview.
B. Read the Major Themes.
C. Read Chapter Eleven in the anthology.
D. Examine carefully Section XI of the Continuity Table.
E. Answer these questions.

1. What avenues of freedom were open to enslaved blacks?
2. Why was the presence of free blacks threatening to a slave society?
3. How were the lives of free blacks influenced by opposing whites?
4. Were nonslave blacks free or quasi-free? Why?
5. How did the then-existing justice system differ in its protection and treatment of whites as compared to blacks?
6. What physical and psychological hardships did free blacks encounter in their efforts to establish economic stability?
7. In which professions and occupations did free blacks realize some success?
8. How did the evolution of free black families differ from that of slave families and of white families?
9. What were the resulting manifestations of increased educational opportunities for free blacks?
10. How was society at large affected by a more articulate and more vocal free black citizenry?
11. What role did free blacks have in western expansion? In American wars?

POSTEVALUATION

To check your learning, select the most appropriate answer to each of the following questions:

1. Which of the following was not a contributing factor in the increase of the free black population?
    a. Revolutionary philosophy of egalitarianism.
    b. Northern prohibition and gradual emancipation.
    c. Manumission by slaveowners.
    d. Excess of free births over deaths.
    e. Slave pardons by governors.
2. Which statement best explains why southerners waged a campaign against free blacks?
    a. To perpetuate control of whites over blacks.
    b. To run free blacks off to the North.
    c. To eliminate job competition presented by free blacks.

    d. To keep free blacks in their place.
3. How did slaveholding states demonstrate their interest in the welfare of free blacks?

    a. Gave them the opportunity to choose their masters and reenslave themselves.

    b. Provided them with jobs of indentured servant status.

    c. Gave them the right to own property and establish a homestead.

    d. None of the above.

4. Which difficulty did *not* affect free blacks born of free mothers in their attempts to establish economic stability?

    a. Legislation barring them from certain trades.

    b. Psychological transition from enslavement to freedom.

    c. Opposition of whites to blacks in the artisan class.

    d. Intimidation and violence directed at blacks to eliminate competition of free blacks.

5. A direct and visible result of increased educational opportunities to free blacks was

    a. a breakthrough of free blacks into some of the large white universities.

    b. an articulate and vocal black citizenry participating in the antislavery movement.

    c. the founding of black colleges and universities.

    d. documentation of black history.

    e. all of the above.

(For correct answers, see ANSWER KEY.)

ANNOTATED BIBLIOGRAPHY

Franklin, John Hope. *From Slavery to Freedom.* New York: Knopf, 1974. Chapter XI on quasi-free Negroes is an extensive treatment of free blacks during slavery. Franklin touches on all the important social, cultural, economic, and political issues which affected free black citizenry.

Smythe, Mabel M., ed. *The Black American Reference Book.* Englewood Cliffs, N.J.: Prentice-Hall, 1976. Contains a brief history of black Americans written by John Hope Franklin. The section on free blacks is good but limited to free blacks in the South and in the North.

Bennett, Lerone, Jr. *Before the Mayflower.* Baltimore: Penguin Books, 1962. Captures in a colorful way the life of the free black. Contrasts economically poor free blacks with economically secure and prosperous free blacks.

CHAPTER TWELVE

ABOLITION: The Antislavery Crusade

One who loves the children of his fellow will surely love his own children. (AFRICAN PROVERB)

OVERVIEW

The idea that America had a mission to bring to the world democracy, freedom, and limitless opportunities gained acceptance quite early in our history. America was to be the new Jerusalem in the wilderness, a beacon of hope for those in Europe and the rest of the world seeking fulfillment of individual aspirations. Many Americans pointed to the achievements of the young nation and were convinced that God was deeply involved in America's destiny. But a few thoughtful men were troubled by inconsistency, a contradiction in philosophy that existed in the nation even before its birth. Slavery was the issue that caused their agony; they commenced working for its abolition, hoping to remove this blemish from the nation's complexion.

Early abolitionists launched an antislavery crusade that in time would help embroil the nation in civil war. Although their protest was becoming organized, its effect upon the general populace was limited and weak. As early as the revolutionary struggle, voices were raised against slavery. Delegates to the Constitutional Convention argued heatedly over statements on slavery, which in the end were eliminated to prevent further dissension among the colonies.

After 1820, the whole of the United States was seized by the reform impulse. Participants in these social movements wanted to reshape America to reflect Christian principles. Temperance societies came into being which condemned the consumption of alcohol as "white slavery." Peace organizations dedicated to pacifist ideals worked for the eradication of war. Women organized and demanded the right to vote. Penal and educational reform groups labored for the reduction of crime and the spreading of the three r's. Even religion was caught up in communistic and polygamous experimentation.

The antislavery crusade was one of the many reform movements of the day. Black and white, male and female, all participated in different organizations simultaneously. Abolitionism, after 1830, overshadowed many of the other activities because its advocates were relentless and vociferous in their attacks, and the moral issue was perhaps more clearly defined. The abolitionists hated slavery not only because it was evil but because it contradicted their basic belief about mankind. They passionately believed in the perfectability of mankind, so the abolitionist's goal could not be compromised—slavery must be dealt a death blow and abolished forever.

In this chapter, the development of the antislavery crusade, from gradualism to militancy, is analyzed; black involvement in the abolitionist struggle is given consideration; and the pros and cons of the slavery debate are examined.

OBJECTIVES

As a result of studying this chapter, you should be able to:

1. Describe the inconsistencies upon which the institution of slavery was based by citing the rationale of the abolition movement.
2. Discuss the effect of militant abolitionism on the antislavery movement by describing the actions of David Walker, William Lloyd Garrison, and Nat Turner.
3. Assess the importance of the underground railroad by describing its role in the abolitionist movement.
4. Discuss the proslavery and antislavery debates by contrasting their views about slavery.
5. Define the goals of the American Colonization Society by describing the activities in which it engaged.
6. Differentiate between gradualism and militant abolitionism by comparing the tactics of each for abolishing slavery.
7. Describe the components of the antislavery crusade by isolating and identifying specific major reform movements.

MAJOR THEMES
GRADUALISM AND RESETTLEMENT

Early abolitionists labored in an atmosphere of rising sectionalism as the United States underwent both the exuberance and the pain of growth and expansion. They believed themselves to be practical men who sought a gradual end to slavery, stressed moderation and cooperation with slaveholders, and refused to engage in incendiary propaganda. They firmly believed that the best way to solve the race problem was to emancipate slaves slowly and to compensate planters for the loss of this human property.

This position, of course, was unacceptable to proslavery factions. They believed that liberation of slaves would create more problems than would continuance of the system. They felt that slaves were not prepared for, or perhaps even capable of, functioning as free persons in a free society; that a body of free blacks within the general population would constitute a threat to whites, in general, and to those still retaining slaves, in particular.

In an attempt to alleviate these fears, the American Colonization Society was formed in 1817. This organization was dedicated to the slow and orderly emancipation of slaves. Once manumitted (freed), former slaves and other free blacks would be resettled in Africa. The Society's publication, *The African Repository,* was full of editorials seeking national support. Such notables as Francis Scott Key, Henry Clay, Andrew Jackson, and Judge Bushrod Washington (George Washington's nephew) were among its first members. For a number of reasons, these efforts achieved only limited success. Despite great expenditures of time and money, the Society had resettled only 15,000 blacks in Africa by 1860.

Black Americans were hostile to the efforts of the Society. Shortly after the formation of the American Colonization Society, nearly 3,000 free blacks were present at Philadelphia's Bethel Church to issue their response. They denounced the Society's program as a vile trick to rid the nation of its free black population. On the other hand, southerners too were suspicious of the organization and gave it little support. Blacks wanted the emancipation of slaves but would have nothing to do with gradualism.

Although the quiescence between 1800–1830 cannot be equated with the stagnation of the abolition movement, the onslaught of militant abolitionism after 1831 gave such an appearance. Even before the attack of militant reformers, many southerners undoubtedly recognized that their defense of slavery was a lost cause. The whole of the Western world was stressing democracy and humanitarian values that ran counter to the "Southern way of life." The gradualists would not remain in the forefront of the abolitionist struggle for long. The South seemed to be at peace with itself; and most Americans, during this lull, were not prepared for the militant abolitionist storm.

MILITANT ABOLITIONISM

Abolitionist newspapers were being established in most cities of the North and the West. These publications were of great importance because they were the primary vehicles for the spread of antislavery propaganda, gaining support for abolition and sometimes creating resentment toward their own cause. In the early days, such papers as the *Philanthropist* (1817), *Manumission Intelligencer* (1820), and *Genius of Universal Emancipation* (1820) served this purpose, but were all moderate in tone, lacking the fervor of the radical literature to come.

In 1829 this radicalism was expressed in David Walker's pamphlet called *Walker's Appeal in Four Articles, Together with a Preamble to the Colored Citizens of the World, But in Particular and Very Expressly to Those of the United States,* often shortened to *Walker's Appeal.* Walker, a free black and a tailor by profession, expressed the view that blacks could achieve their liberation through violence and bloodshed. Some of his pamphlets were found below the Mason-Dixon line. Southern opinion held that the pamphlets were incendiary and that Walker should be jailed. A few months later Walker died under mysterious conditions.

Suddenly, in 1831, William Lloyd Garrison's newspaper the *Liberator* appeared. Garrison, before his conversion by blacks to the cause of immediate abolition, was a gradualist. His first editorial on New Year's Day, January 1, 1831, was brutally frank: "I *will be* as harsh as truth, and as uncompromising as justice. On this subject, I do not wish to think, to speak, or write, with moderation . . . I am in earnest—I will not equivocate—I will not excuse—I will not retreat a single inch—AND I WILL BE HEARD." Garrison made good his promise.

Approximately nine months after Garrison made his dramatic statement, in August 1831, Nat Turner led a bloody insurrection. Turner was a deeply religious man who often had mystical visions, and embarked upon his mission to liberate the slaves believing he was doing God's will. More than sixty white men, women, and children were killed in Turner's insurrection. Fear and terror were widespread throughout the South as news of the event became known.

Walker, Garrison, and Turner marked the arrival of militant abolitionism. Garrison, with the help of blacks, organized the New England Anti-Slavery Society in 1831. As the "Garrisonian" abolitionists grew in numbers, they became more vocal and vituperative in their attacks. They demanded the immediate emancipation of all slaves without compensation to slave owners. The militant reformers attacked southern society as decadent, the slaveholder as evil incarnate, and the national government as corrupt and beyond salvage. Their most acrimonious attacks were aimed at the clergy of the day. But moderate abolitionists found the radicalism of the Garrisonians distressing.

Men such as the Tappan brothers, Theodore Weld, and James G. Birney were moderate in their attacks on slavery but were no less dedicated to the institution's demise. Garrison grew weary of moderation and attempted to seize control of the national American Anti-Slavery Society in 1840. Because Garrison was a staunch believer in women's rights, the national organization wanted nothing to do with his followers, though Garrison did succeed in getting the organization to support the right for women to vote. At the same time he brought about a schism that wrecked the parent body. The dissidents formed the American and Foreign Anti-Slavery Society and worked for the abolition of slavery through political action. The Garrisonians held that U. S. politics were controlled by slaveholders.

BLACK ABOLITIONISTS

Much of Garrison's support in the early 1830s came from the black community. They supported his newspaper, helped him organize the New England Anti-Slavery Society, and introduced him to immediate abolitionism, which was to become his life work. Black Americans were fighting for their rights long before the *Liberator* appeared on the scene.

As early as 1827 John Russwurm and Samuel E. Cornish commenced the publication of the first black newspaper, *Freedom's Journal.* They issued a call for a series of periodic conventions to formulate strategies to deal with the problems of free blacks and slavery. The first editorial stated bluntly that blacks should speak for themselves and attend to their own needs. These conventions met until the eve of the Civil War.

With the rise of militant abolitionism, blacks increasingly supported the antislavery crusade. However, the schism in the abolition movement in the early 1840s produced a twofold result: first, the number of black leaders increased, bringing more aggressive leadership to the forefront; second, these new leaders demanded greater autonomy and became critical of the ideological positions of their white counterparts. Men like Frederick Douglass, Henry Highland Garnet, and Samuel Ringgold Ward became political in their reform attempts. Others commented upon the prejudice of white reformers and argued that this was additional evidence of the need for independent leadership and organization.

The black church was one source of autonomy that for decades provided direction and comfort. Most of the outstanding blacks during the nineteenth century were ministers. The church provided opportunities for leadership that were not available elsewhere because other avenues of advancement were closed to blacks. Afro-American churches welcomed participation in reform activities of all types. Black ministers, regardless of their religious denomination, stood united in the struggle to end slavery.

Afro-Americans who participated in the antislavery crusade were also members of other reform societies (temperance, peace, penal). They were part of the circuit that traveled throughout the North and the West, attacking slavery and supporting other groups. Their eagerness to engage in these activities was to demonstrate that blacks were not inferior to whites, as proslavery propaganda suggested.

The greatest effort of the black abolitionists was their assistance to the underground railroad, a joint effort by blacks and whites to assist runaway slaves. Some whites were planners and guides, but the most famous, an escaped slave, was Harriet Tubman. She brought out of bondage more than 300 slaves, and this feat was so disturbing to slaveowners that a huge reward was offered for her capture. But the conductors were assisted by vigilance committees. In many instances they provided, food, clothing, and shelter to help establish the ex-slave. The most prominent interracial organization was the General Vigilance Committee of Philadelphia. Three hundred or more slaves were given assistance by the New York Committee of Vigilance, the most outstanding of the totally black organizations.

The Afro-American as abolitionist was required to have courage enough to fight the twin evils of American society: the racism of northern society and the enslavement of his brothers and sisters in the South. Frederick Douglass personified the spirit of black abolitionism at its best. Born a slave in 1817 in Talbot County, Maryland, of a slave mother and white father, Douglass started his career, also his escape, in 1838 when he described his experience as a slave to an antislavery audience. As orator, editor, advocate of women's rights, and humanitarian, Frederick Douglass labored to end the institution of slavery.

SLAVERY DEBATE

The debate over slavery was often charged with emotion. Both sides believed in the rightness of their convictions and denounced each other's positions as absurd and dangerous. During the period of gradualism, many southerners apologized for, and sometimes even attacked, the institution of slavery. Southern reaction to militant abolition, however, was a retrenchment in position, asserting that slavery was a positive good. The South felt itself under siege from the harshness of the militant abolitionist attacks.

The opponents of slavery argued that to keep humans in bondage was a sin and a crime. Slavery, for the abolitionists, was sinful because it denied the teachings of Christ and was therefore anti-Christian. To keep the slave in bondage and not pay for his labor was criminal—in short, thievery. The abolitionists also pointed out that slavery was based upon a one-crop system that destroyed the land and kept the people of the South poor and ignorant. If the South were to achieve the same level of development as the North, new ideas and new people (immigrants) would be necessary to give life to a dying civilization.

Many abolitionists wrote pamphlets, organized societies, and circulated petitions in an effort to bring about the moral conversion of the defenders of slavery through a massive propaganda campaign. Becoming aware of the fact that their efforts fell upon deaf ears, some reformers condemned southern society in the most violent language.

The defenders of slavery were not swayed by the abolitionists' attacks. In fact, they answered all the reformers' charges, and gave insult for insult. Many proslavery advocates held that human bondage was not anti-Christian and quoted scripture to validate their position that blacks were inferior to whites and that slavery elevated blacks in ways that were unknown to them in Africa.

Some enlightened men of the South, such as Thomas R. Drew and George Fitzhugh, rushed to the defense of slavery. One view was that most great civilizations of the past, such as Greece and Rome, were built upon slave labor and the South was therefore no exception. In the mid-1850s, publications appeared that stressed the goodness of southern life, the evils faced by northern factory workers, and argued that slaves might be better off because they continued to receive the necessities of life (food, clothing, shelter) from their masters when they became too old to work. The relationship between master and slave was described as a family bond. It was pointed out that there existed in the North a form of *wage slavery* in which white factory workers were degraded and that no one provided for their welfare.

The debate grew more intense as the decade of the 1850s drew to an end. It would take a civil war to end this controversy, but nothing could eradicate the attitudes that the debate over slavery had produced.

LEARNING ACTIVITIES

To accomplish the objectives of this chapter, you should do the following:
A. Study the chapter Overview.
B. Read the Major Themes.
C. Read Chapter Twelve in the anthology.
D. Examine carefully Section XII of the Continuity Table.
E. Answer these questions.
   1. Did the attacks on institutionalized slavery by David Walker, Nat Turner,

and William Lloyd Garrison help or hinder the antislavery crusade?

2. Of what importance was the underground railroad to the abolitionist movement?

3. Which reform movement would you have supported? Why?

4. Why was there so little black participation in the colonization or resettlement effort?

5. What political advantages could have been gained from a merger of the gradualist and militant abolitionists?

6. What were the basic differences presented in the arguments between the proslavery advocates and the antislavery advocates?

7. How could the American Colonization Society have been more successful in its aims?

8. Do you believe that America had a moral mission to bring democracy and freedom to the rest of the world?

POSTEVALUATION

To check your learning, select the most appropriate answer to each of the following questions:

1. Proslavery advocates justified institutionalized slavery on the grounds
   a. that slavery increased the degree of equality between the races.
   b. that God ordained the bondage of Africans.
   c. that the Indians forced southern whites to enslave blacks.
   d. that blacks were inferior to whites.
   e. (b) and (d) only.

2. The editor of the *Liberator*, the radical journal of militant abolitionism was
   a. Frederick Douglass.
   b. David Walker.
   c. Samuel E. Cornish.
   d. William Lloyd Garrison.
   e. none of the above.

3. Colonization as a means of solving the race problem in America stressed
   a. interracial marriages.
   b. establishing a black state in the South.
   c. granting all slaves immediate manumission.
   d. (b) and (c).
   e. none of the above.

4. Militant abolitionists asserted that southern society
   a. was moving toward industrialization faster than the North.
   b. often enslaved poor whites who could not prove that they were free.
   c. was on the brink of interracial harmony because of the increases in mulattoes.

    d. was more religious than northern society because of the South's fundamentalist religious orientation.

    e. none of the above.

5. The leading black abolitionist of the nineteenth century was

    a. David Walker.

    b. Nat Turner.

    c. Frederick Douglass.

    d. William Still.

    e. none of the above.

(For correct answers, see ANSWER KEY.)

ANNOTATED BIBLIOGRAPHY

Barnes, Gilbert Hobbs. *The Anti-Slavery Impulse, 1830–1844.* New York: Harcourt, Brace & World, 1964. A good study of the abolitionist movement. However, the book is marred by the excessive prejudice of the author against the radical reformers. The antislavery activity between 1830–1844 is thoroughly presented.

Cash, J. W. *The Mind of the South.* New York: Vintage Books, 1941. A must for any student who wishes to comprehend southern behavior. Cash traces the historical conditions which shaped the southerners' values and attitudes about slavery, and about black/white relations in general.

Filler, Louis. *The Crusade Against Slavery, 1830–1860.* New York: Harper & Row, 1963. An in-depth analysis of the abolitionist movement and the relationship of the many reform movements to one another. Although the Civil War was not fought to preserve slavery, it was always an element that kept hostilities between North and South alive.

Griffin, S. C. *The Ferment of Reform, 1830–1860.* New York: Crowell, 1967. An excellent introductory account of the variety of reform movements prior to the Civil War which gives a concise analysis of the meaning of reform.

Litwack, Leon F. *North of Slavery: The Negro in the Free States, 1790–1860.* Chicago: The University of Chicago Press, 1961. Another good account of blacks living in free states. The work indicates there was little freedom for blacks in the North.

Quarles, Benjamin. *Black Abolitionists.* New York: Oxford University Press, 1969. The best and most complete book on the subject. Quarles highlights the ideological differences between white and black abolitionists.

Richards, Leonard L. *Gentlemen of Property and Standing: Anti-Abolition Mobs in Jacksonian America.* New York: Oxford University Press, 1970. Richards's volume demonstrates beyond doubt that much of the violence against the abolitionists was directed by the "best" elements of the community, many of whom participated in thuggish activity.

Sweet, Leonard I. *Black Images of America, 1784–1870.* New York: Norton, 1976. An interesting work that provides insight into black thought about America, abolitionism, and the question of black identity. Sweet demonstrates that black leaders during the nineteenth century believed that their mission was to advance the cause of Africans and be the conscience of America.

Tyler, Alice Felt. *Freedom's Ferment: Phases of American Social History From the Colonial Period to the Outbreak of the Civil War.* New York: Harper & Row, 1962. An excellent general volume that covers every major reform activity before the Civil War. The only shortcoming is that there is little analysis of the interrelationships of the various reforms to one another.

McKitrick, Eric L., ed. *Slavery Defended: The Views of the Old South.* Englewood Cliffs, N.J.: Prentice-Hall, 1963.

Thomas, John L., ed. *Slavery Attacked: The Abolitionist Crusade.* Englewood Cliffs, N.J.: Prentice-Hall, 1965. These two volumes provide excellent primary source material on the subject of this chapter. The collected documents contain works of the leaders of the day who fought for or against slavery.

CHAPTER THIRTEEN

CIVIL WAR:
The Beginning of
an Era

Suffering and happiness are twins. (AFRICAN PROVERB)

OVERVIEW

The decade before the Civil War was filled with crises that propelled the nation toward savage conflict. Slavery was part of the growing controversy. The United States had acquired new lands from its conflict with Mexico. Northerners quickly voiced the opinion that slavery should be excluded from the new territories as expressed in the Wilmot Proviso. The South disagreed but knew that slavery had reached its limit of expansion.

The Compromise of 1850 attempted to settle the debate over slavery in the new territories—California entered the Union as a free state and slavery was abolished in the District of Columbia. As a matter of appeasement to the South, the newly implemented Fugitive Slave Act provided slaveowners with the assistance of law officials in returning runaway slaves. In an effort to circumvent the law, nearly 4,000 Afro-Americans left their homes and fled to Canada for safety. The Act aroused hostility in the North, while southerners felt that the law was not being enforced.

In 1852 Harriet Beecher Stowe published *Uncle Tom's Cabin,* which abolitionists applauded and proslavery forces condemned as vicious lies. The popular story formed resentments on both sides of the slavery question.

In 1854, the Kansas-Nebraska Act widened the gap between North and South. The bill, introduced by Stephen A. Douglas, provided that territorial legislatures had the power to decide the slave question in their region. Antislavery and proslavery forces flooded into Kansas, seeking to gain control of the legislators and determine the direction the state would take. A bloodbath erupted.

By the time of John Brown's hanging in December of 1859, Abraham Lincoln was emerging as the Republican choice for president. Although the Republican platform was antislavery, the charge of many southerners that Lincoln was an abolitionist was completely unfounded. As the election results came in from across the nation, it became evident that "Honest Abe" would be the next president. The South, angered, dismayed, and fighting to retain a way of life, determined that there was only one course of action—secession. As Lincoln left Springfield, Illinois, to assume his new duties as President of the United States, the Union was crumbling.

This chapter examines Lincoln's role as the emancipator; the participation of blacks during the Civil War; the conditions that the slaves faced as free people; and focuses upon the reconstruction era and its meaning for black Americans.

OBJECTIVES

As a result of having studied this chapter, you should be able to:
1. Assess the impact of the Compromise of 1850 by describing its effects upon the northern and the southern sections of the country.

2. Discuss Lincoln's proposal for solving the race problem between whites and blacks by describing the components of his preliminary proclamation.
3. Discuss the treatment of black soldiers during the Civil War by contrasting their roles with those of whites in the Union and Confederate armies.
4. State the difficulties that the freedmen encountered during the post-slavery era by describing the hardships they encountered upon being set free.
5. Illustrate the political status of blacks during the Reconstruction era by describing the constitutional benefits of the thirteenth, fourteenth, and fifteenth Amendments to the United States Constitution.
6. Describe the political contributions of Southern blacks by listing the legislation that they helped to incorporate into state constitutions.

MAJOR THEMES
LINCOLN AS EMANCIPATOR

The now famous Lincoln-Douglas debates clearly demonstrated Lincoln's sentiments concerning black Americans. While he stated that the Declaration of Independence included blacks, he did not believe in the social and political equality of the races. Lincoln argued that there was a natural separateness of the races based upon physical differences, and that white prejudice refused to accept blacks, slave or free, as equals. Lincoln, therefore, did not favor giving blacks the right to be voters and jurors.

Lincoln's realism made him aware that the black man's future in America was bleak. Like Thomas Jefferson before him, Lincoln believed that recolonization was the best solution to the race problem. He believed that in Africa (Liberia) or Haiti, the Afro-American had a better chance to try to develop his talents than in America. Lincoln's colonization scheme had no support within the black community.

The preliminary proclamation of September 21, 1862, drafted by Lincoln, called for the gradual emancipation of all slaves, but provided that slaveholding states could delay freedom until 1900. Furthermore, the proclamation provided compensation to slaveholders for the loss of their property. Abolitionists and blacks thundered their disapproval of the President's proposal.

It is difficult to assess whether the events shaped Lincoln, or Lincoln shaped the events. He did not have a plan for making slaves soldiers; he did not enforce the confiscation acts; he believed that his colonization scheme was good; and he wanted to save the Union without emancipating the slaves, if possible. Not long before his death in 1865, however, Lincoln's approach to the slave question and free blacks changed greatly. Blacks, slave and free, were encouraged to join the Union forces. The President felt beyond any doubt that the institution of slavery was evil and must be eradicated.

Any analysis of Lincoln becomes complicated because of his paradoxical beliefs. Lincoln is considered by some to have been a racist and by others to have been one of America's greatest humanitarians. Perhaps he is more deserving of the latter reputation. "Honest Abe" had a tremendous capacity for change, growth, and development.

BLACK INVOLVEMENT IN THE CIVIL WAR

The Civil War did not end as quickly as most northerners had predicted. In fact, the war dragged on for nearly five years. The loss of life on both sides was immense. The conflict took its toll on the manpower and material of both sides, especially the South, where the destruction of its economy left the region impoverished and its people oppressed.

Blacks were eager to join the Union cause. They felt that freedom was near, and wanted to help liberate their brothers and sisters bound in slavery. At the onset of the conflict, black involvement was not wanted. By the end of the struggle (1865), however, more than 180,000 black troops were enrolled in the Union army. These soldiers functioned in all capacities of service, even as spies and scouts. A notable example was Harriet Tubman, who obtained valuable information for the Union as a spy. Blacks also performed many menial tasks.

While the North made use of its black population in direct support of the military effort, the South used its slaves indirectly to support their effort. Early in the conflict, the South suffered from a manpower shortage. White slaveowners left to join the Confederate forces, and slaves stayed on the plantations, where they provided the Confederacy with food. Blacks were also employed in the construction of forts and roads. As the war drew to an end, many southerners even debated the issue of whether slaves should be armed to help win the war. It is doubtful that the South could have fought as long as it did without the support of slave contributions.

Slaves were not paid for their labor in the southern war effort, and the black troops of the North received less money than their white counterparts. Blacks who had the misfortune to be captured by the Confederacy were usually resold into slavery, and were often brutally maltreated. Such were the risks blacks took in order to strike a blow for freedom.

THE SLAVE AS FREEDMAN

All of black America was saddened by the death of President Lincoln in April 1865. Sadness yielded to joy with the news that the war was over. Thousands of black Americans flocked to church and gave thanks to God for liberating them. The realities of freedom, however, soon snapped the freedman's premature optimism. Freedmen now faced the hardships of survival.

Nearly four million slaves had been freed without employment or money. Their difficulties were compounded by "black codes," which prohibited them from living in areas reserved for whites, denied them the right to vote, and made them subject to arrest should they violate vagrancy laws.

Many freedmen began to wander throughout the South in search of relatives. A few freedmen moved northward with the hope of securing a better life for themselves and their families. The vast majority of the freedmen, however, remained in the vicinity of their birth. As a consequence, the master-slave relationship, in many instances, remained firm. The slave's personal adjustment to freedom was not so simple as the change in legal status. The newly freed blacks had to break the bonds of psychological dependence and assert their self-worth. Life for the freedmen was difficult and the future promised more of the same.

The Bureau of Refugees, Freedmen, and Abandoned Lands (or Freedmen's Bureau) provided some minor relief. This government agency was unprepared to handle the complex problems of poverty, disease, education, and the social reconstruction of the South. Its most valuable contributions were in the area of education. Fisk and Howard are outstanding examples of the black colleges that came into existence with the aid of the bureau. The freedmen contributed to the establishment of black education by raising funds for the construction of additional buildings and for hiring needed teachers. Although many of the freedmen did not possess the most basic reading and writing skills, they hungered for understanding. Young and old alike crowded into one-room schools to obtain an education.

In the years to come, freedmen found some relief with the beginning of radical reconstruction. The programs of reconstruction seemed bright and the freedmen looked toward the future with a great deal of hope.

RECONSTRUCTION AND BLACKS

Reconstruction has been described by some scholars as a period of African domination. The years between 1865 and 1877 were full of great achievements and great failures. But at no time during the Reconstruction era did blacks control any states in the South. During this period, many social and political gains were made by blacks. These gains were made possible by the policies of radical Republicans in Congress.

Charles Sumner and Thaddeus Stevens, the two leading radicals, were primarily responsible for the marked change in black status. The Thirteenth Amendment (1865) ended slavery. The Fourteenth Amendment (1868) bestowed citizenship upon blacks. The Fifteenth Amendment (1870) gave black males the right to vote. These constitutional provisions paved the way for wider black participation in southern affairs. One of the most lasting black accomplishments achieved during Reconstruction was the rewriting of state constitutions. These new constitutions outlawed imprisonment for debt; extended suffrage to all males, black or white, over the age of 21; and abolished all property qualifications for voting.

Only two blacks served in the United States Senate during the whole of the

Reconstruction period, Blanche K. Bruce and Hiram Revels, both of Mississippi. Twenty blacks were elected to the U.S. House of Representatives. National black leadership was of high quality, but black officials at the state and local levels were often criticized as being little men in big jobs. Graft and corruption were widespread throughout the South and most politicians, black and white, indulged in thievery.

Many Americans felt that blacks were at last receiving justice, after their long experience of oppression. Reconstruction provided the hope for such optimism. Beneath the surface of the post-Civil War years, however, there were signs of things to come. Blacks still were at the bottom of the southern economy. In many areas of the South, blacks continued to defer to whites as if whites were still masters. The general white population felt that blacks overstepped their bounds and had to be put in "their place". White organizations such as the Ku Klux Klan, the Pale Faces, and the Knights of the White Camellia emerged in an effort to reestablish white domination. With the election of President Hayes, the gains of the Reconstruction era vanished altogether.

LEARNING ACTIVITIES

To accomplish the objectives of this chapter, you should do the following:
A. Study the chapter Overview.
B. Read the Major Themes.
C. Read Chapter Thirteen in the anthology.
D. Examine carefully Section XIII of the Continuity Table.
E. Answer these questions.
   1. What were the issues involved in the Compromise of 1850?
   2. Do you think that Lincoln's colonization proposal to send blacks to Africa was impractical?
   3. Why did blacks work to support the Confederacy during the Civil War?
   4. Could blacks have successfully avoided the "black codes" without federal support?
   5. What made life so difficult for black freedmen during the postslavery era?
   6. What is the political significance of the Thirteenth, Fourteenth, and Fifteenth Constitutional Amendments to both black and white people?
   7. Do you think that Lincoln was a racist? Why? Do you think that Lincoln was a humanitarian? Why?

POSTEVALUATION

To check your learning, select the most appropriate answer to each of the following questions:
1. Slavery, as an issue, was connected with which of the following?

    a. The Compromise of 1850.

    b. *Uncle Tom's Cabin*

    c. The Wilmot Proviso.

    d. All of the above.

2. The foundation of Lincoln's racial views was

    a. the idea that God cursed the black race.

    b. the so-called scientific evidence of the Southern Biological Society.

    c. the idea of separateness of the races.

    d. the absolute equality of the races.

3. The era of Reconstruction can be characterized as

    a. one of black domination.

    b. one of rapid economic growth for the South.

    c. a period of increased activity in the slave trade.

    d. a period of relative equality between blacks and whites.

4. One of the major functions of the "black codes" was

    a. to spread literacy among the exslaves.

    b. to control the black population.

    c. to provide transportation for those blacks who wanted to return to Africa.

    d. to provide guidelines for the construction of black hospitals during Reconstruction.

5. The adjustment of freedmen to emancipation was difficult because

    a. the exslave had to break the bonds of psychological dependence.

    b. of the desire of many freedmen to become masters themselves.

    c. many freedmen believed that America was not their true home.

    d. all slaves wanted to remain in bondage.

(For correct answers, see ANSWER KEY.)

ANNOTATED BIBLIOGRAPHY

Craven, Avery. *The Coming of the Civil War.* Chicago: University of Chicago Press, 1966.
Craven, Avery. *Reconstruction: The Ending of the Civil War.* New York: Holt, Rinehart and Winston, 1969. These two books should be read in sequence. The author gives a balanced account of the Civil War and of Reconstruction. Both are good.

Du Bois, W.E.B. *Black Reconstruction in America, 1860–1880.* New York: Atheneum, 1970. This is the first major work by a revisionist historian on the Reconstruction. Du Bois's volume contains a great deal of information that is left out of newer treatments of this period. The work suffers from a forcing of black/white relations into a Marxist framework.

Logan, Rayford W. *The Betrayal of the Negro: From Rutherford B. Hayes to Woodrow Wilson.* New York: Collier Books, 1965. A fascinating piece of literature that highlights the breakdown of reconstruction and the violence and repression blacks endured from the late nineteenth century to the early twentieth century.

McPherson, James M. *The Negro's Civil War: How American Negros Felt and Acted During the War for the Union.* New York: Vintage Books, 1965. This is a much-needed work that gives a detailed account of the activities of Afro-Americans in the Civil War. As

McPherson makes clear, blacks were critical of Union policies but supported the war 100 percent.

Sinkler, George. *The Racial Attitudes of American Presidents: From Abraham Lincoln to Theodore Roosevelt.* Garden City, N.Y.: Doubleday, 1971. A blunt and straightforward book that deals with some of our presidents' racial attitudes. The book provides new perspectives on why some of the presidents' policies developed the way they did.

Stampp, Kenneth M. *The Era of Reconstruction, 1865–1877.* New York: Knopf, 1965. One of the best revisionist histories of the Reconstruction period. Students will find this work easy to read and highly informative. Stampp deals with all the old issues of Reconstruction, but his interpretation is alive and critical.

CHAPTER FOURTEEN

POLITICAL COMPROMISE: The Nadir of Black Americans

The wise person who does not learn ceases to be wise.
(AFRICAN PROVERB)

OVERVIEW

The Compromise of 1877 brought an end to the Reconstruction era and to black political and socioeconomic gains. The period after 1877 has been described as the lowest point of historical existence for black Americans. Blacks were forgotten by their former Northern supporters, rejected and physically intimidated by southerners, overlooked by the U. S. Supreme Court, and politically powerless in national affairs.

Two black men dominated black libertarian thought during the latter stages of the nineteenth century and into the twentieth century. Booker T. Washington advocated a philosophy of industrial training and working with one's hands. Dr. W. E. B. Du Bois supported an educational philosophy of higher education, intelligence, and knowledge of the world.

During the ensuing years, black Americans, even though disfranchised, developed their own institutions of higher learning and their own social hierarchy. The black quest for equality would continue into the twentieth century.

This chapter describes the negative impact of the Compromise of 1877 upon blacks in the South. The chapter also focuses upon the two giants of black libertarian thought during the late nineteenth and early twentieth centuries.

OBJECTIVES

As a result of having studied this chapter, you should be able to:
1. Discuss improvements for blacks during the Reconstruction period by describing their political gains.
2. Determine the impact of black officeholders on state governments by describing the kind of positions they held.
3. Analyze the impact of the election of 1876 by examining the disputed elections in Florida, South Carolina, and Louisiana.
4. Evaluate the political effects of the Compromise of 1877 on blacks by examining the political compromise that southern whites were able to extract from President Hayes.
5. Identify the terror tactics of southern whites by describing the activities of the Ku Klux Klan and similar organizations.
6. State the methods of disfranchisement that southern whites used by describing their tactics for preventing blacks from voting.
7. Determine the impact of Jim Crow laws on black and white Americans by examining the institutions that banned or segregated black Americans.
8. Describe the educational philosophies of Booker T. Washington and Dr. W. E. B. Du Bois by contrasting their philosophies on the objectives of higher education for blacks.

MAJOR THEMES

BLACK POLITICAL GAINS DURING THE RECONSTRUCTION ERA

Black people in the South made significant political and economic strides during the Reconstruction period. Twenty-two black men served in Congress between 1869 and 1901, including two senators, Hiram Revels and Blanche Kelso Bruce, both representing the state of Mississippi. Six blacks were elected lieutenant governor in Mississippi, South Carolina, and Louisiana. Francis L. Cardozo, a graduate of the University of Glasgow, served as state treasurer of South Carolina. Jonathan Gibbs, a graduate of Dartmouth College, was superintendent of education for the state of Florida.

The significant gains of the Reconstruction era began to disappear, however, after the election of 1876. In that disputed election, Rutherford B. Hayes, the Republican nominee, received 48 percent of the vote; the Democratic nominee, Samuel Tilden, received 51 percent of the vote.

The election returns in South Carolina, Florida, and Louisiana were disputed by both candidates, each claiming victory. The dispute was taken to the House of Representatives in Congress. Southern Democrats were willing to accept Hayes if he agreed to pull federal troops out of the South and allow the southern states to manage their internal affairs by themselves. Hayes agreed, and the future of former slaves became very dismal.

THE POLITICAL COMPROMISE OF 1877

This Compromise of 1877 brought reconstruction to an end. The period following 1877 marked what one historian has aptly called "the nadir" of the history of black people in the United States. Blacks and their descendants were condemned, in the interest of sectional harmony, to lives of poverty, indignity, and little hope. Meanwhile, the rest of America continued its golden march toward wealth and power.

EXTRALEGAL AND ILLEGAL METHODS OF ELECTORAL INTIMIDATION

The Knights of the White Camellia, the Pale Faces, the White Brotherhood, and the Ku Klux Klan were used by southerners extralegally or illegally to exercise absolute control over blacks in the South. Armed with swords and guns, the Ku Klux Klan began to run blacks out of communities if they disobeyed orders to desist from voting. If the blacks refused to run, they were whipped, maimed, or hanged. If violent methods failed to deter blacks from voting, then extralegal devices such as literacy tests, poll taxes, or white primaries were used to purge millions of blacks from the election rolls of the South.

Also, for those blacks who were allowed to vote, the politicians would supply plenty of barbecue, whiskey, and fish for those who voted the "right" way. By 1910, the pattern of extralegal and illegal disfranchisement was complete. Blacks had been successfully purged from the election rolls of Mississippi, South Carolina, Louisiana, North Carolina, Alabama, Virginia, Georgia, and Oklahoma. For example, in 1896 there were 130,344 blacks registered in Louisiana. In 1900, only 5,320 were on the registration books. Of 181,471 black males of voting age in Alabama in 1900, fewer than 3,000 remained on the rolls in 1910.

The Creation of "Jim Crow"

Dan Rice was a famous blackface minstrel. In 1830, on a street in Cincinnati, Ohio, he saw a small ragged black child singing and dancing "Jump Jim Crow." Dan Rice copied the song and dance and used it in his minstrel shows. The words eventually became synonymous with the de jure separation of blacks from whites in education and recreational institutions in the South.

Beginning in Tennessee, the first of the South's "Jim Crow" laws was enacted, and the rest of the South followed suit. Blacks and whites were thereafter separated on all modes of transportation. Blacks were banned in hotels, restaurants, and theaters. By 1885, most southern states had laws requiring separate schools for black children and white children. These segregation laws were upheld by the U. S. Supreme Court in the infamous case of *Plessy* v. *Ferguson*. The court ruled that if facilities for the two races were equal, it was not discrimination if they were separate.

Frederick Douglass had provided unchallenged leadership in black libertarian thought for almost half a century, until his death on February 20, 1895. Fortunately, as history has shown, new leaders often emerge to add momentum to important movements. In the later nineteenth and twentieth centuries, Booker T. Washington and W. E. B. Du Bois assumed this leadership and thereby achieved permanent status in American educational and philosophical thought.

THE EDUCATIONAL PHILOSOPHY OF BOOKER T. WASHINGTON

Booker T. Washington had worked his way through Hampton Institute, a black college in Hampton, Virginia. He received an education which emphasized practical, industrial training by working with one's hands. Washington frowned upon formalized education because he believed it to be divorced from everyday life. A masterful orator, he was successful in getting Alabama whites to supply financial support for the new school that he founded, Tuskegee Institute, in Tuskegee, Alabama.

He also gained financial support from northern philanthropists in developing

The philosophical conflict between Booker T. Washington and Dr. W. E. B. Du Bois was best described in a poem by Dudley Randall (From *Poem Counterpoem,* copyright © 1966, by Dudley Randall. Reprinted by permission of Broadside Press):

Booker T. and W. E. B.

"It seems to me," said Booker T.,
"It shows a mighty lot of cheek
To study Chemistry and Greek
When Mister Charles needs a hand
To hoe the cotton on his land,
And when Miss Ann looks for a cook
Why stick your nose inside a book?"

"I don't agree," said W. E. B.,
"If I should have the drive to seek
Knowledge of Chemistry or Greek,
I'll do it. Charles and Miss can look
Another place for hand or cook.
Some men rejoice in skill of hand,
And some in cultivating land,
But there are others who maintain,
The right to cultivate the brain."

"It seems to me," said Booker T.,
"That all you folks have missed the boat
Who shout about the right to vote,
And spend vain days and sleepless nights
In uproar over civil rights.
Just keep your mouths shut, do not grouse,
But work, and save, and buy a house."

"I don't agree," said W.E.B.
"For what can property avail
If Dignity and justice fail.
Unless you help to make the laws,
They'll steal your house with trumped-up clause.
A rope's as tight, a fire as hot,
No matter how much cash you've got.
Speak soft, and try your little plan
But as for me, I'll be a man."

an educational endowment which was bigger than any other black college and most Southern white colleges then had. Washington and his students made the bricks, built the buildings, constructed the furniture, grew the crops, and raised the livestock for the school.

Washington took ignorant, backward blacks, living in abysmal poverty as cotton sharecroppers, and taught them how to improve their lives through cleanliness, industry, thrift, diversified farming, family budgeting, and family planning. Tuskegee Institute gained an international reputation for its work, and people from all over the world came to learn its ways of educating people.

George Washington Carver served on the Tuskegee faculty from 1896 to 1943. His creations in agriculture enriched all the South and benefited both black and white southerners. Dr. Carver developed synthetic products out of peanuts, sweet potatoes, and soybeans. He also pioneered in the process of dehydrating foods for longer preservation and less bulky shipping.

Booker T. Washington was accepted by the white power structure in the South because of his views on segregation. In his Atlanta Compromise speech of September 18, 1895, Washington told an audience of 40,000 cheering whites and crying blacks that in all things that are purely social, we can be as separate as the fingers—flinging his outstretched hands above his head—yet one, as the hand, in all things essential to mutual progress.

He also told the audience that blacks should withdraw from politics, start at the bottom of the economic ladder and work their way to the top, and gain political equality by economic success as craftsmen, businessmen, and professionals for a subsequent rise to first-class citizenship. After this speech, white Americans selected Washington as the official leader of the black Americans.

THE ALTERNATIVE EDUCATIONAL PHILOSOPHY OF W. E. B. DU BOIS

Booker T. Washington's foremost opponent was W. E. B. Du Bois. He was educated at Fisk University, Harvard University, where he received the degree of Doctor of Philosophy, and Berlin University. While teaching at Atlanta University in Atlanta, Georgia, Du Bois did research on the conditions of blacks in the South. He wrote books, essays, and addresses opposing what he considered to be the narrow educational philosophy of Booker T. Washington. *Souls of Black Folk,* which Du Bois wrote in 1903, criticized Washington's *Gospel of Work and Money* as a philosophy which negates the higher aims of life.

In an essay entitled "The Talented Tenth," Du Bois said, "If we make money the object of man training, we shall develop moneymakers but not necessarily men. If we make technical skill the object of education, we may possess artisans but not men. Men we shall have only as we make manhood the object of the work of the schools. Intelligence, broad sympathy, knowledge of the world that was and is, and of the relation of men to it, this is the curriculum of that higher education which must underlie life."

Du Bois became an eloquent spokesman for the growing numbers of black intellectuals, who began to attack Booker T. Washington's leadership of the black people.

During the years after the Compromise of 1877, black Americans, though disfranchised, created their own institutions of higher learning and their own cultural life. Blacks developed a social structure similar to, but separate from, the dominant white culture. The black quest for equality was to lead to racial conflicts in which more than 3,000 blacks were lynched. Discrimination would dog blacks' footsteps but would not prevent black libertarians from reminding white America that all persons are created equal.

LEARNING ACTIVITIES

To accomplish the objectives of this chapter, you should do the following:
A. Study the chapter Overview.
B. Read the Major Themes.
C. Read Chapter Fourteen of the anthology.
D. Examine carefully Section XIV of the Continuity Table.
E. Answer these questions.
   1. What political concessions did the southern Democrats gain from the Compromise of 1877?
   2. What was the impact of the Compromise of 1877 on the political and socioeconomic status of blacks?
   3. What were some of the extralegal and illegal acts of disfranchisement by which southern politicians eliminated blacks from the voting rolls of the South in 1877?
   4. What legal criteria were used by the U.S. Supreme Court to justify Jim Crow laws in the South? Also, what socioeconomic institutions were most affected by Jim Crow laws?
   5. After examining the educational philosophies of Booker T. Washington and W. E. B. Du Bois, which philosophy do you think black people should have preferred?

POSTEVALUATION

To check your learning, select the most appropriate answer to each of the following questions:
1. Which of the following black leaders did not hold a congressional or state office before the election of 1876?
   a. Hiram Revels.
   b. Frederick Douglass.
   c. Blanche K. Bruce.
   d. Francis L. Cardozo.
   e. Jonathan Gibbs.
2. In return for their votes in the House of Representatives, Rutherford B. Hayes made which of the following political concessions to southern politicians?
   a. Southern leaders were given the power to try federal troops for any violations in state courts.

    b. Military governors could no longer exercise exclusive powers.

    c. Federal troops were allowed to remain in the South.

    d. Southern politicians were given the power to control their internal affairs without interference.

    e. All of the above.

3. Of the following, which was not a post-Reconstruction white terrorist organization?

    a. Knights of the White Camellia.

    b. The Pale Faces.

    c. White Brotherhood.

    d. White Citizens Council.

    e. Ku Klux Klan.

4. The U.S. Supreme Court case in which Jim Crow laws were used to segregate the races in educational and recreational institutions was called:

    a. Scott v. Stanford.

    b. Plessy v. Ferguson.

    c. Marbury v. Madison.

    d. Condon v. Herboy.

    e. Smith v. Alwright.

5. The educational philosophy of Booker T. Washington emphasized

    a. technical education.

    b. family planning.

    c. diversified farming.

    d. painting and mending.

    e. all of the above.

(For correct answers, see ANSWER KEY.)

ANNOTATED BIBLIOGRAPHY

Bracey, John, August Meier, and Elliott Rudwich. *Black Nationalism In America.* New York: Bobbs-Merrill, 1970. A collection of readings vividly describing the libertarian writings of black nationalists in the history of America.

Emanuel, James, and Theodore Gross. *Dark Symphony. Negro Literature In America.* New York: Free Press, 1968.

Morsbach, Mabel. *The Negro In American Life.* New York: Harcourt Brace, 1966. This is an interesting and illustrated book on the contributions of blacks to this country.

Twombly, Robert. *Blacks In White America Since 1865.* New York: David McKay, 1971. This anthology provides the reader with the original writings of black libertarians from 1865 to contemporary times. The selections of Booker T. Washington and Dr. W. E. B. Du Bois provide the reader with a vivid account of their philosophical conflict.

CHAPTER FIFTEEN

AMERICA: A Cultural Exchange

You change your steps according to the change in the rhythm of the drum. (AFRICAN PROVERB)

OVERVIEW

There is a generally accepted historical rule that the roots of a national culture are found in its soil and among the people who have worked it. America is no exception. Blacks have historically been a part of America's peasantry and in this role have had considerable influence on American culture at large. The intent of this unit is to examine, in historical sequence as well as in topical fashion, both the folk and the formal contributions of the black American to American culture. Those contributions have been in every area of American life—in politics, labor, education, religion, recreation, art, music, and so forth. America would not be as it is today were it not for the significant physical and cultural contributions of blacks.

Historically, contributions stretch out over a wide span of time and a variety of social conditions but divide easily into two phases. The first is the period of slavery; the second is a postslavery period in which contributions continue to be made. Slavery was a crucial dilemma. Its resulting problems and resolutions were the basis for many events in American history and for some of the most characteristic qualities of American culture. Slavery represented generations of mutually dependent contact between blacks and whites. The domestic character of the American slave system caused these contacts to be close and often intimate. There was an outer show of social distance and social untouchability, yet there was also a reciprocal cultural exchange. Southern society provided the base for a subtle and often unrecognized effect of blacks upon American culture. The postslavery phase is much more extensive and varied, and gives perhaps a more accurate picture of the interaction of black culture with the rest of American culture.

This unit identifies the contributions of blacks to American culture in the areas of language, folklore, music and dance, art, economics, industry, expansion, and democracy. It does this by isolating and identifying contributions made before, during, and after slavery.

OBJECTIVES

As a result of studying this chapter, you should be able to:
1. Discuss the development of American culture by describing the exchange that took place between black and white Americans.
2. Recognize that some developments in American culture were dependent upon slavery as an institution by identifying those areas where slavery had an impact.
3. Describe the transfer of African heritage to American culture by identifying African retentions in American culture.
4. Discuss how blacks have continuously contributed to the evolution of American politics, by identifying specific contributors and their areas of contributions.

5. Assess the impact that black contributions to American culture have had on your life by identifying your habits, thoughts, and actions that have been directly molded or made possible by these contributions.

MAJOR THEMES

AFRICAN RETENTIONS IN LANGUAGE AND FOLKLORE

Africans brought their own culture to the New World. Most of that culture was lost but much of it survived. Survival of Africanisms is most easily found in the culture of black Americans. However, many African retentions are inherent in American culture at large.

No African language is spoken in America today. Historically, Africans who spoke the same language were separated from one another to suppress insurrections. There are, however, verbal and nonverbal examples of African communication carryovers in American culture. Examples include the following:

1. The nonverbal sounds Americans use to say "yes" (um hum), "no," and "I don't know."
2. Certain exclamatory sounds which indicate delight or disgust such as "umph, umph, umph!", smells good "um," smells bad "um" with different intonations.
3. Intonations of exclamatory words (the manner and the style of the exclamation rather than the words themselves are African survivals) "lawd!", "chile."
4. Carryovers of specific words from various African languages, including goober nut, gumbo, tote, yam, okay (or OK), jitterbug, jazz, dig, honkie, and so forth.

Africans came to this country with their own language patterns. They learned the English and French vocabularies and often used them according to the dictates of their own language patterns. This carryover is quite evident in American pidgin and Creole. Examples:

1. In several African languages, urgency is expressed by repetition. In Wolof, the word "now" is *leegi,* pronounced "legi." Consequently, to express "right now" in Wolof, one says *leegi, leegi.* In pidgin English this feeling of urgency is expressed by saying "now, now."
2. In several African languages no distinction is made between the letter "L" and the letter "R." Consequently, "fried" potatoes in pidgin becomes *flied* potatoes.
3. Few African languages have a *th* sound; consequently, "that" and "those" become *dat* and *dose.*

There are Africanisms, too, in American folklore. American classics such as Uncle Remus and the Tar Baby stories are of West African origin. There has not been much transformation. These stories have maintained plot, sequences, and events identical to those in West African folklore.

AFRICAN RETENTIONS IN ART

African art has played a major role in the development of modern Western art. Africans brought many of their artistic ideas with them to the New World, but the American art world failed to recognize them until events in Europe changed attitudes toward African art. Picasso, Braque, Modigliani, and other European artists of the early twentieth century were struck by the powerful rhythms, abstract forms, and artistic vision of African art in the ethnological museums of Europe. By incorporating African ideas into their own work, these painters initiated the Cubist movement and revolutionized the course of modern art.

The influence of African art is clearly apparent in American painting and sculpture. Many modern American artists use forms which are consciously or unconsciously African in origin. Many artists radically simplify and distort the human figure, as African artists did to make it more expressive of their vision. Many modern artists use "interior" space in their sculpture, in a fashion reminiscent of some African sculpture. Mural painting on the outside walls of buildings is an African custom being revived in American cities today by black and white artists.

AFRICAN RETENTIONS IN MUSIC

Africanisms are easily seen in black American music. There have been retentions in song and dance. Even more important, music has been functional in black America just as it was in Africa. Music has served as a means by which blacks could transcend the drudgery and unpleasantness of their existence.

In American music both song and dance often include Africanisms. African polyrhythms are the foundation of American jazz, with its intricacies, repeated themes, syncopations, embellishments, and improvisations. As with African music, no two renditions of an American jazz piece are alike; the performers have the freedom of individual interpretation and embellishment; thus, the music is alive for the performer and the listeners.

American songs, particularly spirituals, show traces of Africanisms in rhythm and vocal style. The "call-response" and "leader-chorus" songs prevalent among American spirituals are direct African carryovers.

Traces of Africanisms are found also in American dance, particularly those dances which feature a combination of active head-and-hand, body-pelvic movements. Interestingly, the American Charleston is nearly identical to an Ashanti ancestor dance.

BLACK AMERICAN CONTRIBUTIONS: EXPLORATION

Black contributions to the development of America began not with slavery but with the first arrival of blacks in the New World. Initial contributions were presumably in exploration of the Americas, when Pedro Alonzo Nino, in the fifteenth century, explored America, sailing to the New World with Columbus. Estevenico, also in the fifteenth century, explored America's southwestern territory. Jean Baptiste du Sable founded present-day Chicago.

BLACK AMERICAN CONTRIBUTIONS: THE ECONOMY

The black contributions did not begin with slavery, but slavery, when it came, was a major factor. Blacks endured; by the simple act of survival, blacks made an inestimable contribution to posterity. Most of the contributions black laborers made to the development of the South are obvious; they cleared lands, planted crops, built houses and cities. Black laborers made possible the existence of the leisure class which produced George Washington, Thomas Jefferson, and other Southern leaders. In short, the labor of blacks facilitated development of the Southern economy and culture. Black laborers made a less obvious, but nonetheless quite substantial, contribution to the economic and industrial development of the North.

BLACK AMERICAN CONTRIBUTIONS: INVENTIONS AND DISCOVERIES

Black Americans, through their inventions and scientific discoveries, have contributed still further to the economic development of America. Blacks received more than 5,000 patents, ranging from machine guns and electronic devices to methods of utilizing atomic energy. Selected examples of black inventions that have affected daily American life are these:
1. Granville T. Wood's telephone transmitter.
2. Jan Matzeliger's shoe-lasting machine.
3. Garret Morgan's traffic lights and gas mask.
4. Norbert Rillieux's sugar evaporating machine.
5. Dr. Charles Drew's process for the utilization and storage of blood plasma.
6. Dr. Daniel H. William's pioneer work in open-heart surgery.

This list barely scratches the surface of the thousands of black inventions or discoveries. The reason why so little knowledge about them exists is that blacks, for a long time, were denied patents. As a result, many ideas were either sold or given to whites who could get patents, and who also got the credit for the contributions of blacks.

BLACK AMERICAN CONTRIBUTIONS: DEMOCRACY

In the republic established by the founding fathers, the franchise was extended only to those who were free, male, and property owners. Therefore, slaves, women, children, and men who did not own property were not allowed to vote, and were, in general, considered incapable of assuming the full responsibilities of

Contributions of blacks to American culture are innumerable. Benjamin Banneker, astronomer and mathematician, wrote a dissertation on bees; he constructed what was probably the first American-made clock. A Georgia slave was in part responsible for the invention of the cotton gin. Jo Anderson helped Cyrus McCormick develop his reaping machine. Morbert Rillieux invented a vacuum cup which revolutionized the sugar refining industry. Elijah McCoy of Detroit received more than fifty patents for devices concerning telegraphy and electricity. Jan E. Matzeliger created the shoe-lasting machine. Matzeliger's patent was purchased by the United Shoe Machinery Company of Boston. It reaped millions of dollars, but Matzeliger died in obscurity.

citizenship. Blacks, through resistance, eloquence, and persistence, have helped America move closer to its professed ideals and basic principles. Selected examples of blacks and their contributions to the building of democracy include the following:

1. Toussaint L'Ouverture established Haiti as an independent black-ruled state, causing Napoleon to give up his idea of an American empire.
2. Crispus Attucks, Peter Salem, Salem Poor, and many hundreds of others fought in the American Revolutionary War.
3. Frederick Douglass struggled throughout his life for the rights of blacks.
4. Sojourner Truth exemplified the role of blacks in the Women's Suffrage movement.
5. Black Reconstruction officials supported the Fourteenth and Fifteenth Constitutional Amendments.
6. W. E. B. Du Bois's contributions include the Niagara Movement, NAACP, and his writings.
7. Martin L. King, Malcolm X, leaders of SNCC, CORE, and so forth.

The black contribution to democracy has been not only in the civil rights movement, but also in combat for America in foreign and domestic wars. Black people fought and excelled in every war America has known. Black soldiers were motivated with double consciousness. They fought to oppose the so-called enemy of their country and for justice for all black people.

1. In the Revolutionary War and the War of 1812, the American black hoped to gain freedom from bondage. He thought if he put his life on the line for this country, he would surely gain his freedom.
2. In the Civil War, he fought in the hope that, as a reward, he would gain his freedom.
3. In the Spanish-American War of 1898, he showed concern over American involvement abroad by fighting gallantly, hoping America would open its doors to him when he returned; it didn't.
4. World War I saw the black man in segregated units, receiving less pay and

Lucy Terry

Popular songs attributed to blacks, such as "Roll, Jordan, Roll" and "Swing Low, Sweet Chariot," were not the first attempts at verse by blacks in the United States. An Indian raid on the Massachusetts town of Deerfield in 1746 was documented in couplets by Lucy Terry, a semiliterate slave girl. It was called "Bors Fight."

> August 'twas the twenty-fifth
> Seventeen Hundred Forty-Six
> The Indians did in ambush lay
> Some very valiant men to slay
> The names of whom I'll not leave out
> Samuel Allen like a hero fout
> And though he was so brave and bold
> His face no more shall we behold.

Nothing else by Lucy Terry survived, and little is known of her interest in verse, but she may well have been alive in Massachusetts when Phillis Wheatley was brought from Senegal in 1761, and a decade later "A Poem by Phillis, A NEGRO GIRL in Boston, on the Death of the Reverend George Whitefield" was published.

Paul Lawrence Dunbar

A son of former slaves presented in 1896 *Lyrics of a Lowly Life,* a book which won for him a national reputation. Helped by the minstrel tradition, Dunbar's popularity was at first based on poems written in the dialect of plantation folk. Others of his writings are in the tradition of Robert Burns, treasured by literate black Americans who emerged from plantation slavery. Many of Dunbar's writings have never been out of print, including dialect poems that made him famous. Others of his poems are in standard English. Some provided the lyrics for songs that remain well known and loved. "Dawn" is an example (from Anna Bontemps, "The Black Contribution to American Letters: Part I," in Mabel M. Smythe, ed., *The Black Reference Book,* Englewood Cliffs, N.J., Prentice-Hall, 1976, p. 747).

> An angel robed in spotless white
> Bent down and kissed the sleeping night.
> Night woke to blush; the sprite was gone.
> Men saw the blush and called it Dawn.

performing menial jobs, away from the front lines where he might receive too much recognition and too much honor.

5. World War II was, for him, practically a repetition of World War I.
6. The Korean conflict saw the black man in integrated units, but treatment of him was the same in Korea as it was when he returned home: oppressed.
7. Vietnam saw the highest percentage ever of black soldiers fighting on the front

lines for America and not for themselves, because upon their return home, they still had to fight discrimination and oppression.

BLACK AMERICAN CONTRIBUTIONS: THE ARTS

Many contributions have already been identified in this area, in the discussion of African retentions. A significant black contribution has been made to American letters. Blacks and black-white relations have long been the subject of much great American literature by white authors, including *Huckleberry Finn* by Mark Twain, novels of William Faulkner, *Uncle Tom's Cabin* by Harriet Beecher Stowe, poems by Walt Whitman, essays by Ralph Waldo Emerson, and so forth.

Black writers themselves have contributed enormously to American letters. Lists of contributions of black poets, playwrights, novelists, historians, essayists and others are long and impressive.

When Europeans and others speak of American music, they commonly think of spirituals, jazz, and rock. In short, they think of black American music. Black

---

James Weldon Johnson

A contemporary of Dunbar was James Weldon Johnson. Johnson was known mainly for his pop song lyrics, including "Lift Every Voice and Sing," which since its composition in 1900 has become the national anthem for black Americans (© Copyrighted: Edward B. Marks Music Corporation. Used by permission).

> Lift ev'ry voice and sing,
> Till earth and heaven ring,
> Ring with the harmonies of Liberty;
> Let our rejoicing rise
> High as the list'ning skies,
> Let it resound loud as the rolling sea.
>
> Sing a song full of the faith
> That the dark past has taught us;
> Sing a song full of the hope
> That the present has brought us;
> Facing the rising sun of our new day begun,
> Let us march on 'til victory is won.
>
> Stoney the road we trod,
> Bitter the chast'ning rod,
> Felt in the days when hope unborn had died;
> Yet with a steady beat,
> Have not our weary feet
> Come to the place for which our fathers sighed?

musicians have given modern American music its form, its direction, and its "soul."

Blacks have contributed to the development of American drama. The improvised plantation entertainment of slavery days, the dancing, the singing, the grinning were the beginnings of a major form and tradition of the American theater: the blackface minstrel and vaudeville.

A substantial part of native American art, in all its various forms, was of black origin. Much of this art, including sports, is in the category of entertainment. It is strange that the segment of our population most subject to oppression and its sorrows has furnished so large a share of the nation's joy and relaxation.

LEARNING ACTIVITIES

To accomplish the objectives of this chapter, you should do the following:
A. Study the chapter Overview.
B. Read the Major Themes.
C. Read Chapter Fifteen in the anthology.
D. Examine Section XV of the Continuity Table.
E. Answer these questions.
   1. How were slaves and whites mutually dependent despite social distance and social untouchability?
   2. What are incidents and examples of the reciprocal cultural exchange that took place between whites and blacks?
   3. Why were the overwhelming majority of laborsaving devices invented by blacks?
   4. Which black contributions to American culture owe their origin to the attempt of blacks to cope and survive under an oppressive system?
   5. What words, or nonverbal expressions, do you commonly use that are of black origin?
   6. Do you recall childhood stories which are either of African origin or which parallel African folktales?
   7. Can you identify specific examples, such as songs or musical pieces, that contain Africanisms?
   8. What have been the contributions of blacks to American culture as a whole?
   9. How would your daily life, including all thoughts and actions, be different if the black contributions to American culture were removed?
F. (Optional) Answer these questions based on the *Roots* story:
   1. When did Kunta meet people or find himself in situations that immediately reminded him of Juffure?
   2. What devices did Bell, Kunta, Chicken George, and Tom create or invent to make their lives and work easier?
   3. What did the slaves on slave row do in their leisure time?

POSTEVALUATION

To check your learning, select the most appropriate answer to each of the following questions:

1. The domestic and rural forms of slavery necessitated group contact between whites and blacks that
   a. generated mutually dependent living.
   b. was very close and often intimate.
   c. encouraged reciprocal cultural exchange.
   d. all of the above.
   e. none of the above.

2. The contrived comic side of blacks in slavery was the genesis of which major form of American theater?
   a. Tragicomedy.
   b. Minstrelsy and vaudeville.
   c. Comedy.
   d. Satire.

3. Black contributions to the development of the United States
   a. began during slavery.
   b. were exclusively in the field of entertainment and sports.
   c. had most impact in the sciences.
   d. all of the above.
   e. none of the above.

4. Black contributions to the economic development of the United States made possible
   a. the exploration of the southwest territory.
   b. the founding of present-day Chicago.
   c. participation in American wars.
   d. the establishment of a Southern leisure class.
   e. all of the above.

5. Little is known about the number or extent of black inventions and discoveries because
   a. most blacks would not reveal to whites their discoveries and inventions.
   b. whites kept the records and did not record inventions and discoveries made by blacks.
   c. ideas or inventions were sold or given to whites because blacks could not get patents.
   d. blacks had little time to concern themselves with inventions.

(For correct answers, see ANSWER KEY.)

ANNOTATED BIBLIOGRAPHY

Butcher, Margaret Just. *The Negro in American Culture.* New York: Knopf, 1956. Easily read, heavily documented book. Successfully attempts to trace in historical sequence the folk and formal contributions of the American Negro to American culture.

Herskovits, Melville J. *The Myth of the Negro Past.* Boston: Beacon Press, 1969. An attempt to dispel stereotypes and myths that exist about the history of black Americans; good section on African retentions in American culture.

Smythe, Mabel M., ed. *The Black American Reference Book.* Englewood Cliffs, N.J.: Prentice-Hall, 1976. Excellent. Brings together in one volume a comprehensive view of the world of black Americans. Outstanding sections on black involvement and contributions to American culture.

ANSWER KEY TO POSTEVALUATION QUESTIONS

Chapter One	Chapter Two	Chapter Three
1. c	1. d	1. c
2. d	2. e	2. b
3. a	3. b	3. b
4. c	4. a	4. e
5. c	5. b	5. d

Chapter Four	Chapter Five	Chapter Six
1. b	1. b	1. e
2. b	2. a	2. a
3. d	3. a	3. e
4. a	4. a	4. b
5. a	5. b	5. c

Chapter Seven	Chapter Eight	Chapter Nine
1. c	1. e	1. e
2. d	2. a	2. b
3. e	3. c	3. e
4. e	4. e	4. b
5. d	5. d	5. e

Chapter Ten	Chapter Eleven	Chapter Twelve
1. e	1. e	1. e
2. c	2. a	2. d
3. b	3. a	3. e
4. c	4. b	4. e
5. b	5. e	5. c

Chapter Thirteen	Chapter Fourteen	Chapter Fifteen
1. d	1. b	1. d
2. c	2. d	2. b
3. d	3. d	3. e
4. b	4. b	4. d
5. a	5. e	5. c

NOTES

NOTES

NOTES

NOTES

NOTES